AF412201

Contents

Introduction

Valentin Carron made his Swiss Institute debut in 2006 at our space on 495 Broadway with his solo exhibition *DÉCHÉANCE, ÉLÉGANCE, DÉHANCHEMENT*, which translates to "Decline, elegance, sway." The show, his first in New York City, introduced his singular approach to dismantling the collectively fabricated mythologies of his home country. His sculptures, equally aggressive, humorous, and solemn, investigate the way we generate histories and how we reconcile the consequences of these cultivated narratives. Over the past ten years, Valentin has continued to develop these themes in his work across media. In early 2014, given his perceptive affinity for dissecting visual culture, Swiss Institute invited him to curate an exhibition. *Work Hard* marks his curatorial debut.

As Valentin describes in this book, *Work Hard* was conceived as a self-portrait; his presence is visible at every turn. From Mai-Thu Perret's *Black Balthazar* (2013) to Fabrice Gygi's *Tente-Bar* (1997), each work elucidates the concepts and concerns that inform his artistic practice. The title is sourced from a graffiti message that adorns a relief by Pierre Blanc in Lausanne, of a shepherd guiding a bull to slaughter, and as one progresses through the show, the phrase "work hard" assumes a multiplicity of meanings. The works engage with a peculiar Swiss vernacular, creating a narrative surrounding national identity and the production of artworks. What Valentin has created is a personal and discerning exploration of Helvetic approaches to art and labor.

More broadly, *Work Hard* furthers Swiss Institute's examination of the artist as curator. Included in this book is a 2013 essay by Kunsthalle Basel director Elena Filipovic, "When Exhibitions Become Form: On the History of the Artist as Curator," which inaugurated *The Artist as Curator* series published by *Mousse* magazine. On the occasion of the exhibition, Swiss Institute invited a panel, moderated by Filipovic, that included the artists Josh Kline, Jennifer Chan, and Leah Schrager. Using Filipovic's essay as a touchstone, the panel focused primarily on the decisions artists make when they set out to curate an exhibiition, and the subsequent complications.

For the exhibition, Valentin has included a 2007 work by
Denis Savary entitled *Alma (After Kokoschka)*. The work is a
recreation of a life-size doll made in 1918 by Oskar Kokoschka,
fashioned in the likeness of Alma Mahler (the love of his
life) on the occasion of her marriage to Bauhaus founder Walter
Gropius. Considering the themes of decay and resistance to death
at play in the work of Savary and his predecessor Kokoschka,
Swiss Institute invited art critic and philosopher Boris Groys
to introduce and screen his video lecture *The Immortal Bodies*.
His presentation is published here in essay form.

This book also includes extraordinary new essays from Valentin's
Swiss comrades, artist Mai-Thu Perret and Fri Art artistic
director Balthazar Lovay. Perret offers her unique insights
on the exhibition, melding Valentin's biography with a broader
historical perspective in relation to selected works in the
show. In "Some Unknown Portraits of Old Friends," Lovay mirrors
Valentin's atmospheric, unorthodox approach to portraiture. His
characterizations, focused more on minutiae than on explanatory
devices, complement Valentin's particular approach to probing
national identity and desire to circumvent an easily accessible
representation.

Spanning over a century, *Work Hard* is a chronologically expan-
sive exhibition, and it could not have been realized without
the willingness and generosity of the artists and lenders.
I thank them for bringing Valentin's ambitious idea to fruition
and creating opportunities for these works to be seen in a new
context. For many of these artists, *Work Hard* has provided
an opportunity to expose their work to New York audiences for
the first time; it is with great pride that Swiss Institute
has given the first presentation in a New York institution
for artists Vittorio Brodmann, Claudia Comte, Sylvain Croci-
Torti, Frédéric Gabioud, Mathis Gasser, Andreas Hochuli,
Simon Paccaud, Denis Savary, and art brut visionary Marguerite
Burnat-Provins.

And, of course, I must express my immense gratitude to Valentin
for his sharp insights and his contagious, relentless commitment to self-doubt. His incisive perspective on his country,
along with his ability to integrate appropriation tactics with
sculptural bravado, speak directly to a core tenet of Swiss
Institute's mission to explore the international relevance of
a national viewpoint.

    Simon Castets
    Director, Swiss Institute

Walk-through with Valentin Carron

Work Hard is really a self-portrait using the art of others. When I look back at the works I chose for the exhibition, I think they are all pieces I would have liked to have made myself, and I put them together as if I were curating a show of my own work. So in a way, *Work Hard* is a form of appropriation. But to be honest, there was no predetermined concept. For all intents and purposes, I made sentimental choices based on gut feelings, and I had no idea where that would lead me, but my passion for the beautiful loser is evident throughout. I really respect failed attempts. Some pieces I knew I wanted to include because they were important to me and have touched me since I've been making art myself. Other works were by artists with whom I wanted to collaborate. I see this exhibition as an overview of Swiss art but without a clear chronological trajectory, and without a formal path, either—I had no desire to do a historical exhibition. In terms of common points among the artists, you could talk about a "Swissitude," but finally this wasn't very interesting to me. I wanted to destroy classifications, so I picked works that didn't have very much in common with one another. I included artists from different generations, of different outlooks and disciplinary backgrounds. A knowledgeable art audience will no doubt know Jean Tinguely, for example, but probably not Simon Paccaud, who just got out of art school. That's what I wanted. There was an interval of a year between when Simon Castets asked me to curate the exhibition and when we actually had to install it, so I had time to mull everything over. In the end, I chose a selection from friends, artists I admire, and things I encountered throughout the year.

I only found the central feeling of the show once everything was gathered together. Normally, when I install a show, I try to expand on the tensions and relationships between the works, and in the space. At Swiss Institute, I assembled things little by little. First I had to decide where to divide the gallery, and how to prepare it to receive the works. I already had ideas about the connections I would make, but I needed to see everything together before it was clear how the works would function as a whole. I wanted to create a sense of coherence and cohesiveness, despite the generation and reputation gaps between the artists, and I thought a lot about how to achieve that balance. I was concerned about how the audience would move through the space, so I made the show in a pretty closed way, building two little walls about ten feet high in order to help forge links between the individual works. I was also concerned about the staging—not about the individual pieces, but rather about the mise en abîme they would create together. We wondered how we would link everything together. I thought, *Well, we can't, but we could have a unifying paint color.* The choice of color for the walls was totally spontaneous: one day I went to smoke a cigarette outside and noticed that Swiss Institute was painted silver, and I told Simon that this would be the perfect color. That's really what happened. There is something about the nature of silver that is relatively neutral.

In general, art always strains between positivism and reformism. In this exhibition, the works are torn between these opposites, or maybe they are at a tangent in the middle. This will to idealize, and also the deep faith it takes to make something, are what I'm attracted to. This reminds me of Baudelaire's *Le Spleen de Paris* (1869). *Spleen* is a French word that roughly describes affect and idealism as the two nipples of modernity. All the works have this desire, this impulse, this drive, but behind this, underneath it, there is always the implication of failure, the fact that things go wrong. It is this contradiction and simultaneity that I'm drawn to.

This dichotomy is present in the title of the show, *Work Hard*, which comes from a phrase graffitied on a sculpture by Pierre Blanc of a shepherd leading a beast to slaughter. What is sort of comical, and at the same time not at all funny, is that during World War II there was fascism in Italy and Nazism in Germany, and, caught in the middle, between the two, was neutral Switzerland. And then this sculpture suddenly appeared in front of a slaughterhouse in Lausanne in the 1950s. It's a bit fascistic, a kind of totalitarian sculpture that refers to Romulus and Remus and the Capitoline Wolf. It is a great glorification of work and man and virility, and man's dominion over the animal. The phrase "work hard" graffitied on the sculpture is in fact a form of found art, because it is an anonymous tag that was added later. It acts as an affect, bringing a contradiction to the sculpture, allowing it to go above and beyond what was there initially. It says "work hard," but also, "feel free to commit idle acts."

pp. 9, 90, 92: Mai-Thu Perret, *Black Balthazar*, 2013

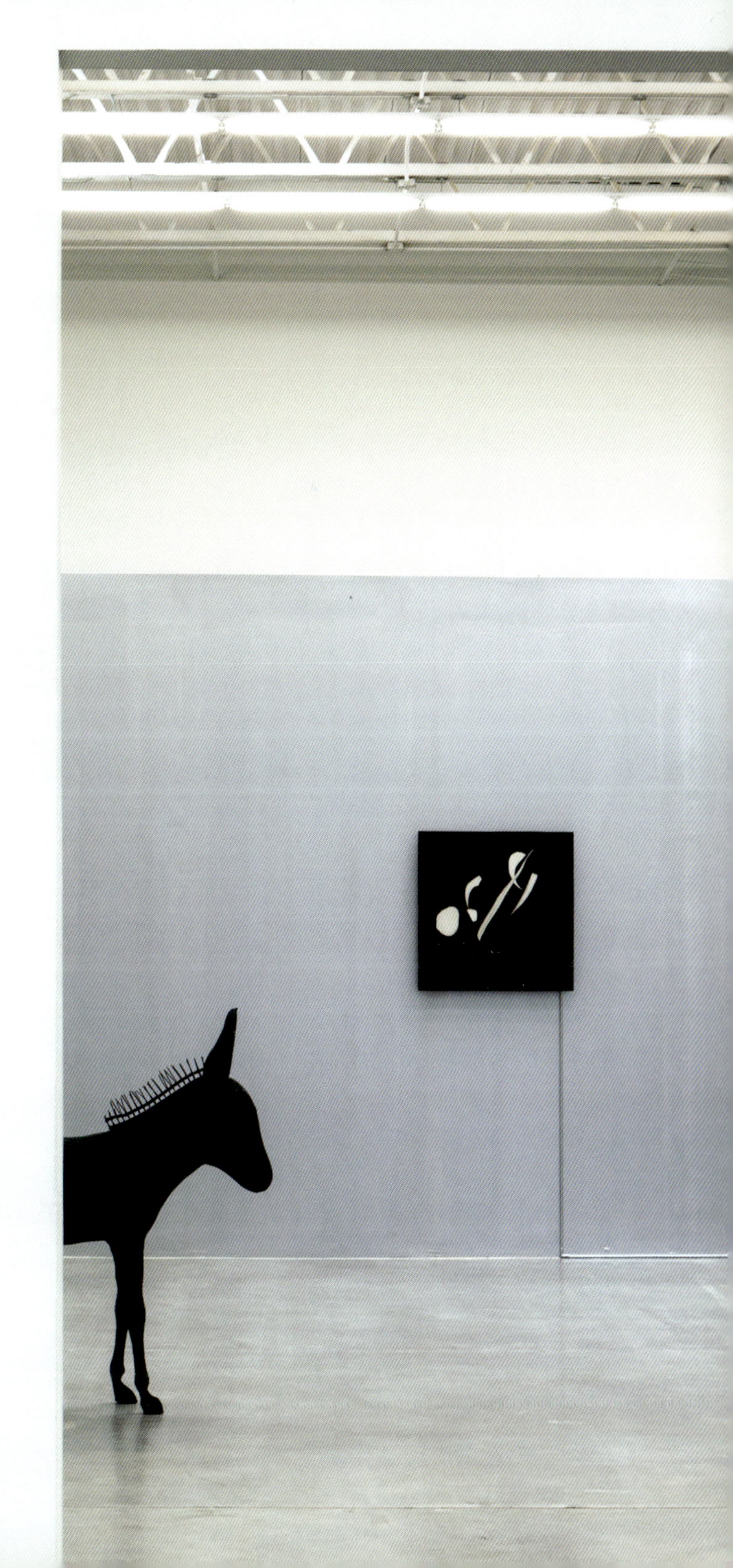

In many ways, *Work Hard* is a representation of the twentieth
century. Edmond Bille, for example, an artist from Fully, which
is my region, published a satirical newspaper during the First
World War called *L'Arbalète*. It was more or less a leftist
paper—anti-military but also anti-pacifist. I'm not a huge
admirer of his paintings, but I appreciate the engravings
from Bille's series

> *Une danse macabre*, 1919
> Folio book
> 19¾ × 13¾ × ¾ inches
> pp. 11-14

The one that touches me most is *Civilisation*, in which the
factories are in the background and the base of a cross and
Jesus's legs are in the foreground. Although there was only
room for a few of the engravings, you can see that the series
was a critique of the horrors of the war. But, I guess, since
they were printed after the war ended, you could say Bille was
a little late. I don't think we realize anymore the magnitude
of the violence of both World Wars—meticulously organized violence. During the first few months of the First World War, two
or three thousand people were killed each day, on all sides.
A hundred thousand were killed every month. Thankfully, a hundred years later, everything has changed. We wouldn't stand for
that kind of carnage anymore. Now, if a French soldier dies in
Afghanistan, he gets a state funeral that the President feels
obligated to attend.

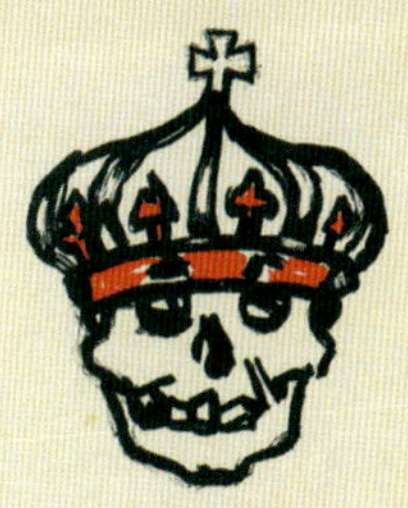

une
Danse macabre

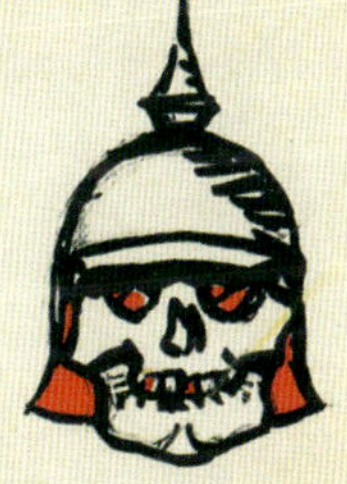

20 GRAVURES EN COULEURS PAR
Edmond Bille

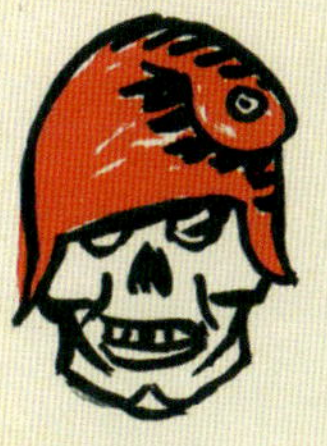

EDITIONS SPES LAUSANNE

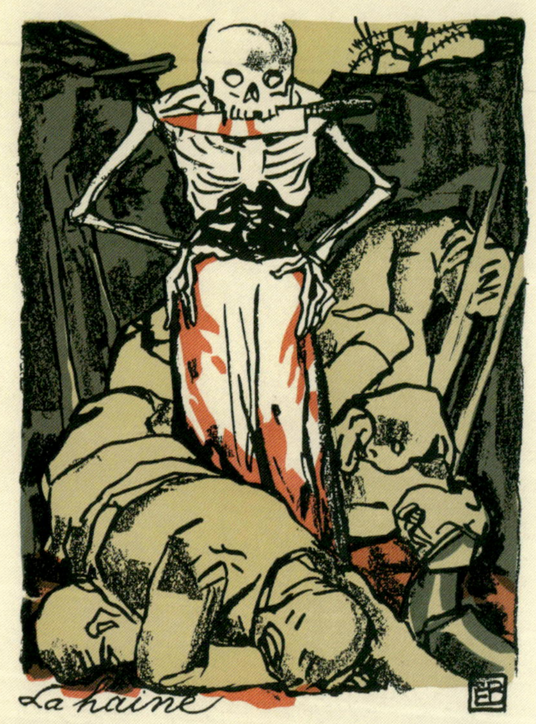

La haine

CINÉMA
RESTAURANT
Rumeurs guerrières

1

Mensonges

11

14

l'autre veilleur

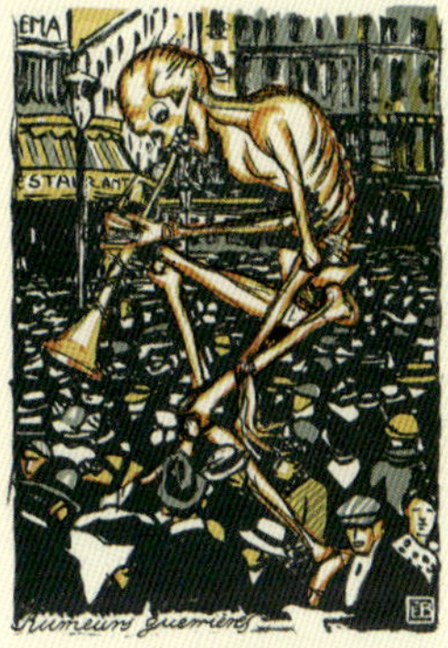

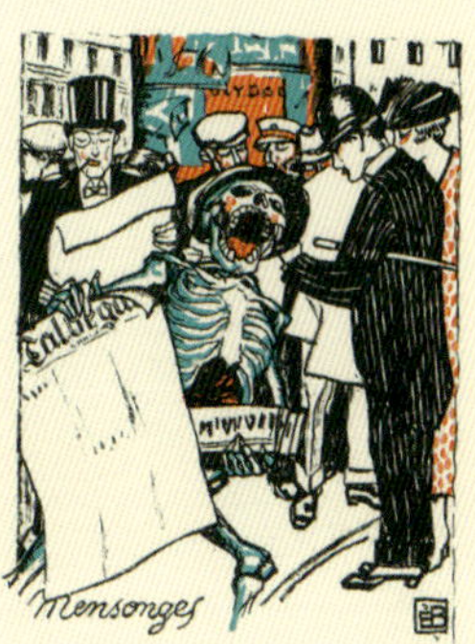

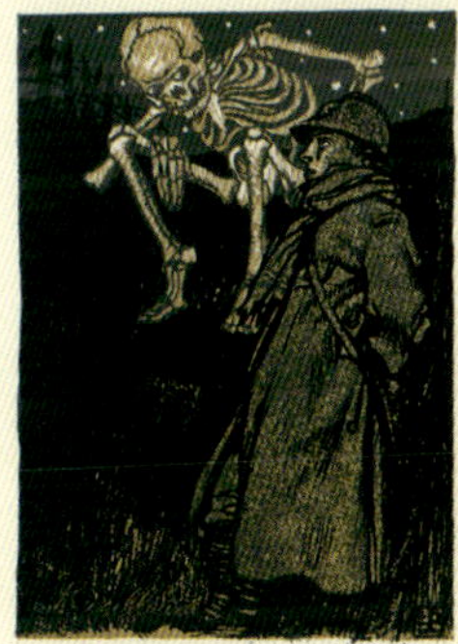

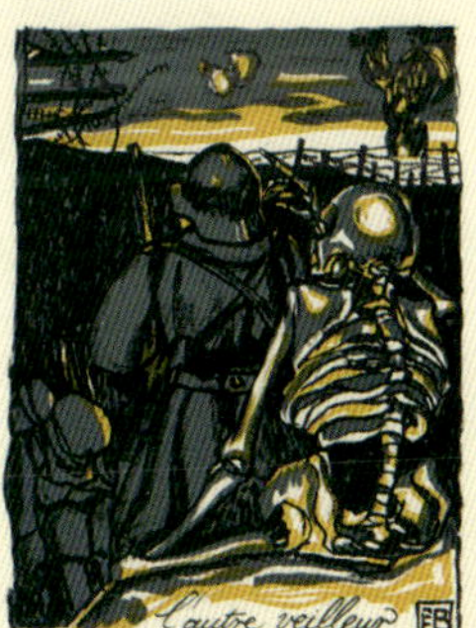

15

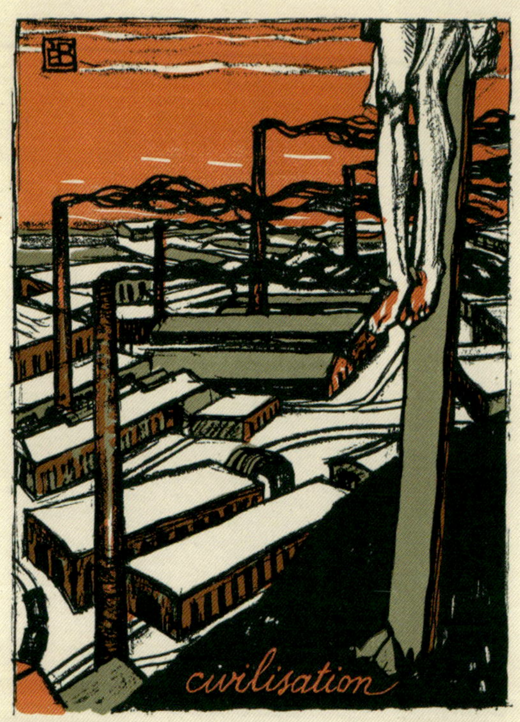

civilisation

I see a connection between *Une danse macabre* and Latifa Echakhch's hyperrealist social sculpture

> *Skin*, 2012
> Shoes
> Dimensions variable
> pp. 16–17, 72

This work is made from shoes her brother collected from his friends and evokes "skin parties," or parties where there are no limits and anything goes. It reminds me of Wolfgang Tillmans's photos of squalid apartments, but when I chose it, I was thinking about George Bellows's *River Rats* (1906). This painting from the turn of the century depicts children jumping into the East River beneath massive earthworks and under-construction piers in Brooklyn. It was painted when American art first started to have a social function and echoes the kind of realism of Victor Hugo. The relationship between the title and the subject is very provocative; it's double-edged. I think those kids were called river rats, and that's what Bellows wanted to highlight. It's the same kind of social critique I find in Echakhch.

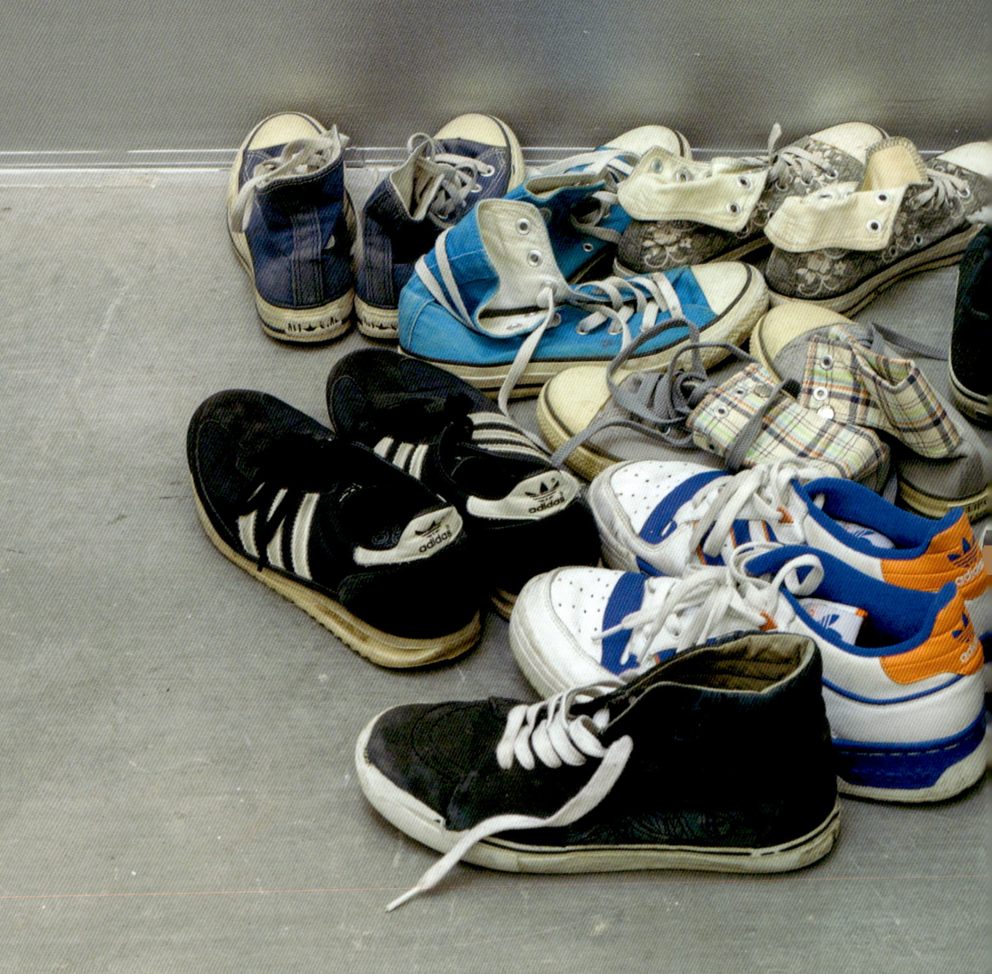

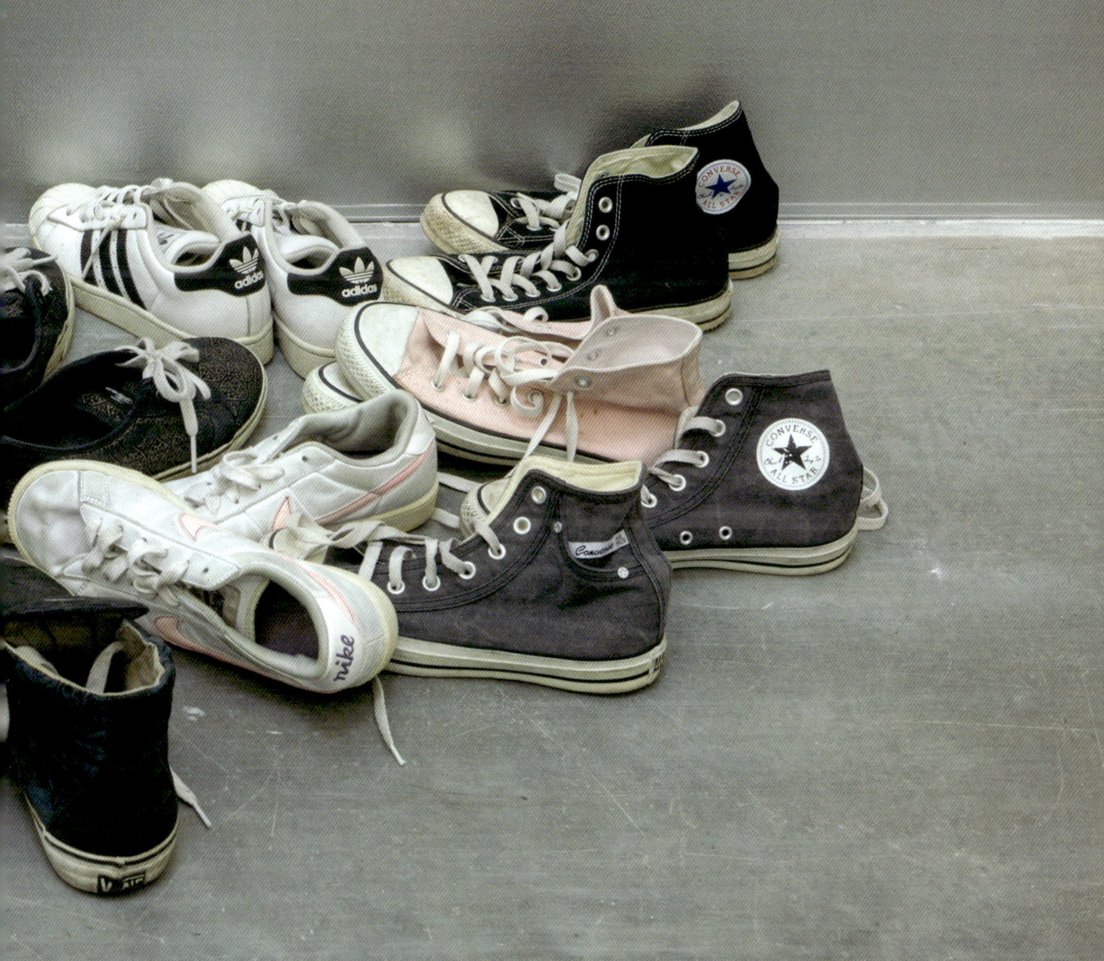

Sometimes there are generational connections in the exhibition,
for example between Daniel Spoerri's

> *Le danger de la multiplication*, 1971
> Mixed media
> 39½ × 39½ × 4 inches
> pp. 19, 74, 114

and Bernhard Luginbühl's

> *Modell zum Karlsruher Stengel*, 1968
> Iron
> 40¾ × 33½ × 13 inches
> p. 20

Then there are also generational gaps, like between Tinguely
and Paccaud. Very early on in the process, Tinguely spoke
loudly to me. There is something eminently Swiss about this
piece. I find it symbolic of what happened in Europe after the
hangover of World War II, when art took off in a positivist
direction. Like Jean Arp, who was a little bit on the fence
between constructivism, surrealism, and formalism, all of a
sudden Tinguely declared that these movements were not suffi-
cient. He could have said, "Oh, I'll just make white forms on a
black background and be done with it," but he didn't. He wanted
to push the limits, and he did. He motorized it. In Tinguely's

> *Peut-être No. 11*, ca. 1959
> Metal mobile relief, motorized
> 24 × 19¾ × 8 inches
> pp. 9, 21-3, 72, 91

shapes move on the frame. And it's impressive. This way of
putting movement into the composition was a kind of sudden
activation, which could have not worked, but it did. Since the
forms move constantly, the composition is never the same,
so the movement becomes a kind of ever-changing construction.
This piece was made around 1959, so it's extremely modern.
It's both of its time and beyond.

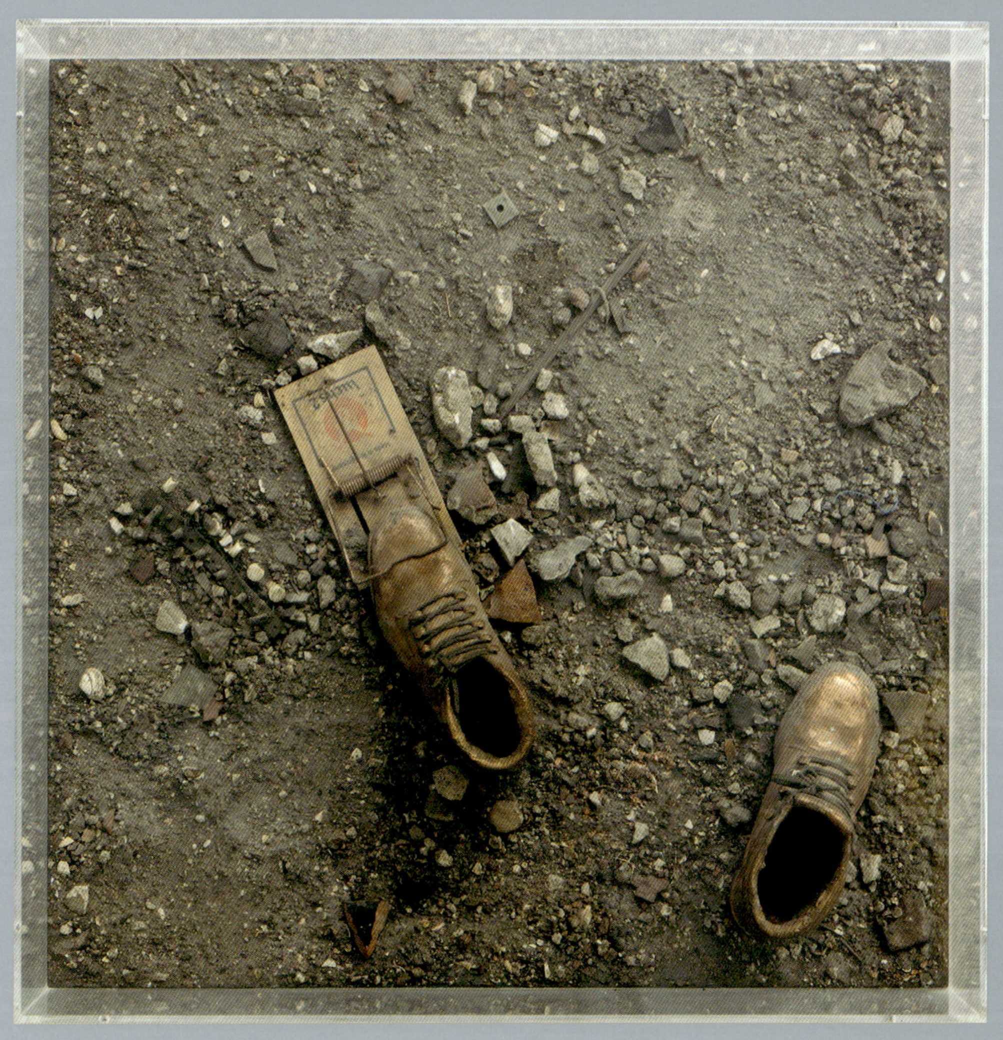

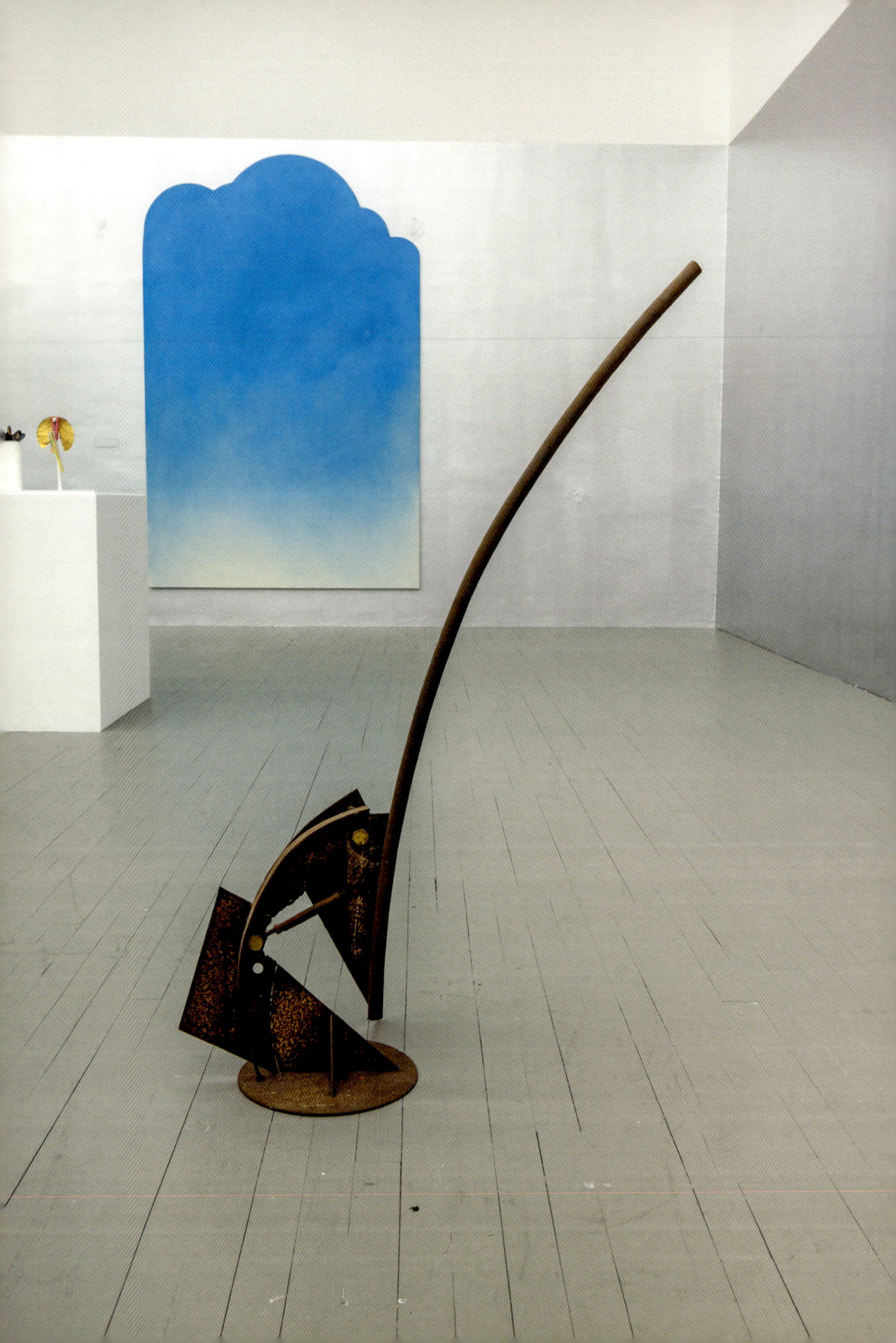

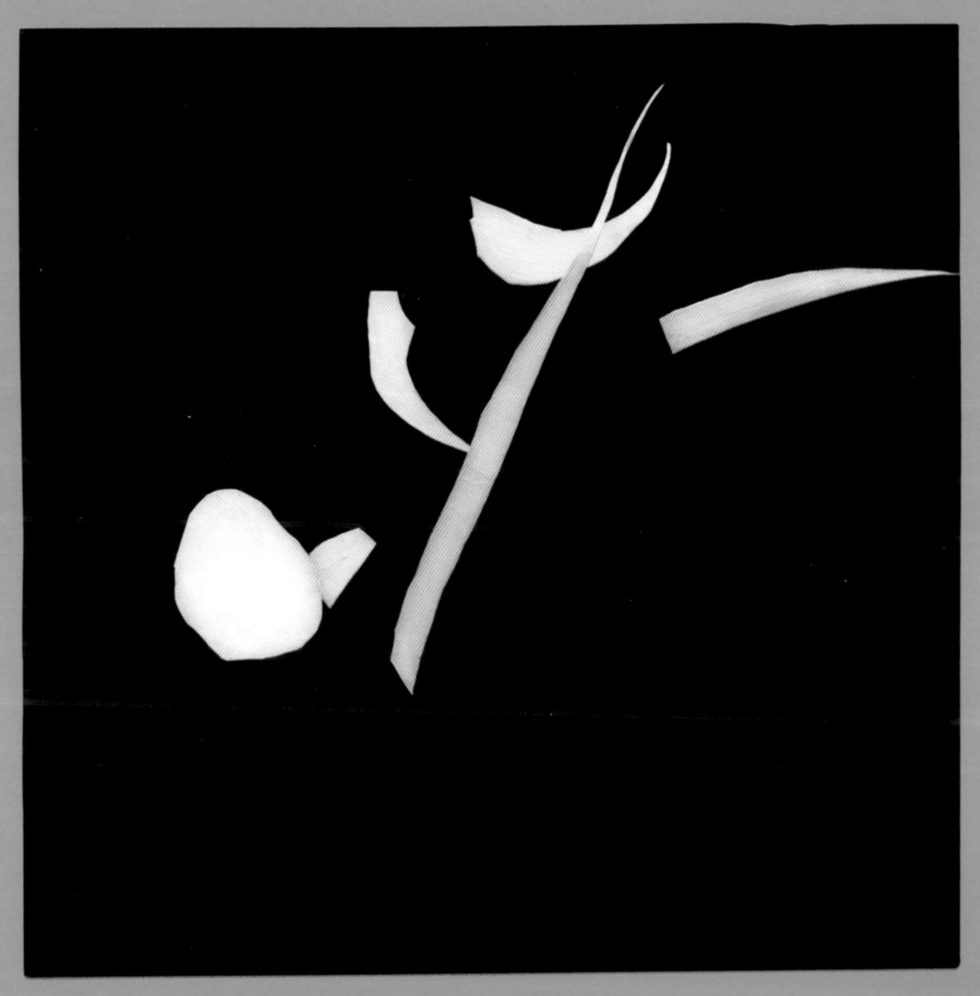

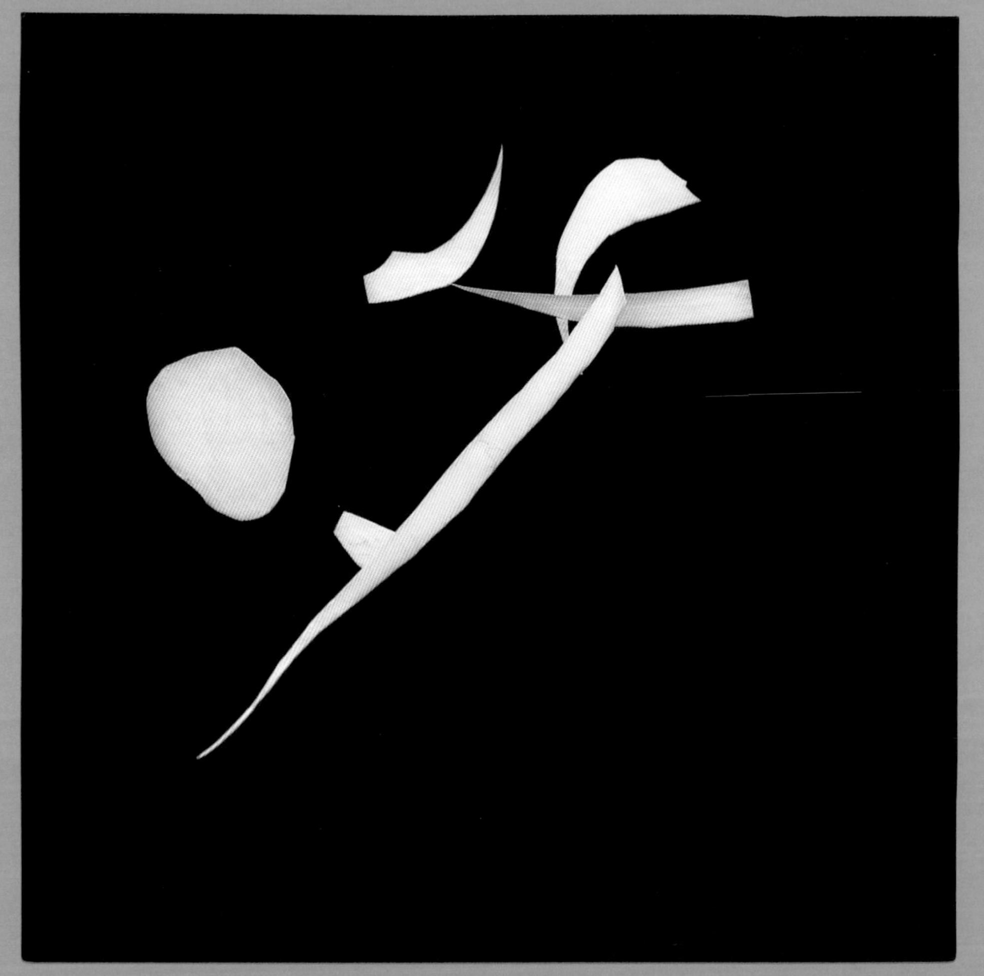

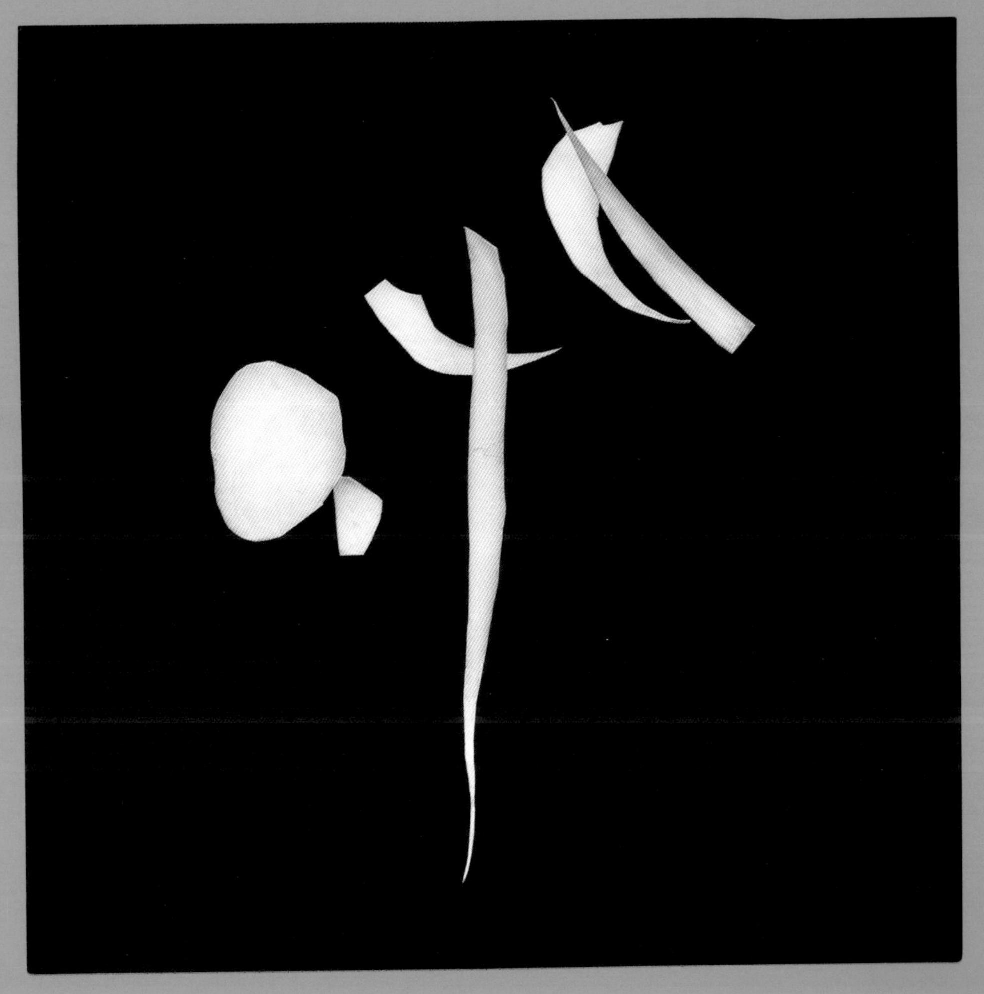

In a different room from *Peut-être No. 11* is the mobile by the young Swiss artist Simon Paccaud,

> *Crocodile*, 2012
> Caps, crowbars, canes, and lace
> 118¼ × 59¼ × 1¼ inches
> pp. 25, 72

I found the contrast of the old people's canes and collection of Lacoste hats interesting and relevant to the modern, ever-changing construction of Tinguely. *Crocodile* is somehow a very disappointing and deceitful way of showing a mobile; in a way it's a failure, but it was my attempt to make an intergenerational connection, even though I didn't understand the canes.

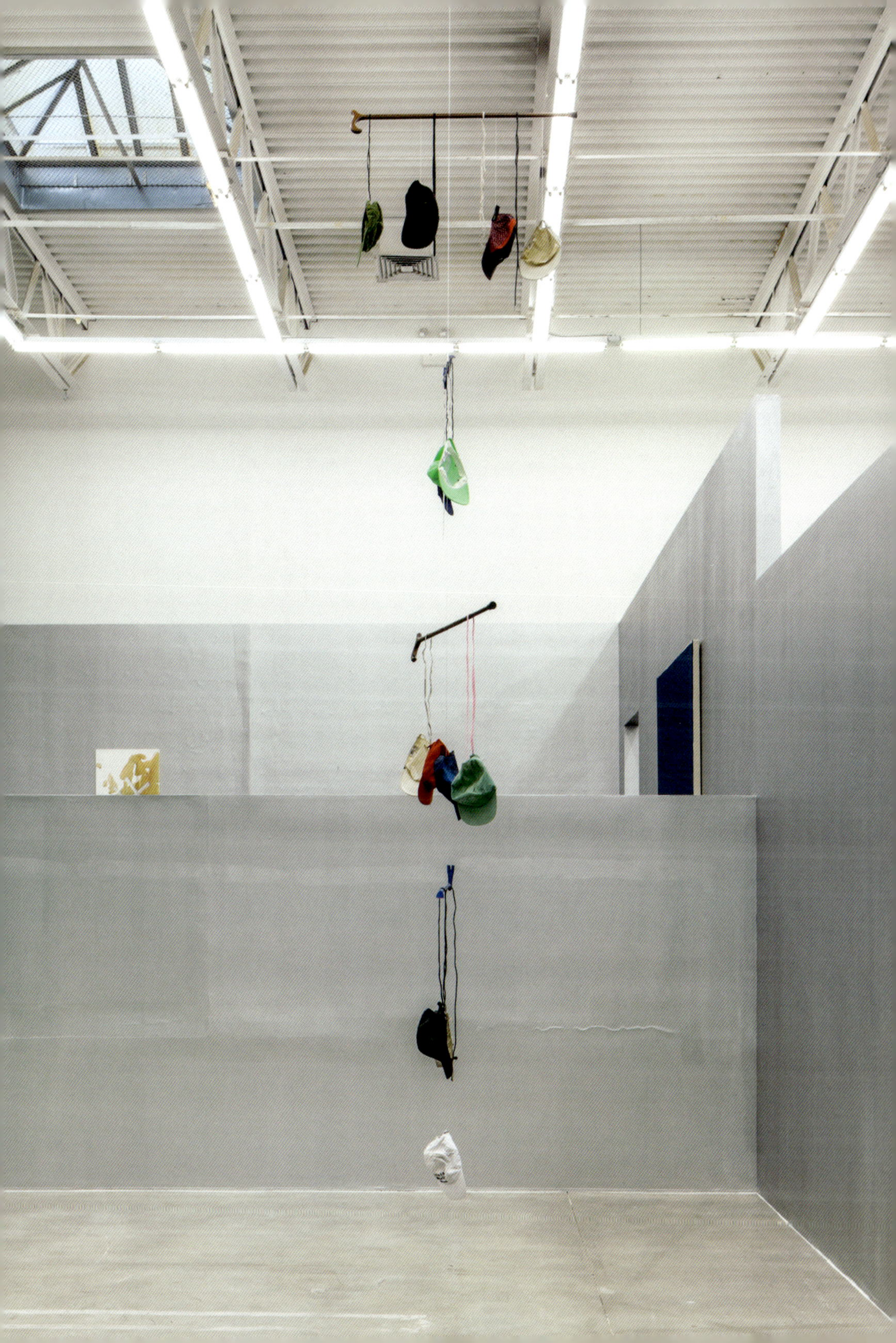

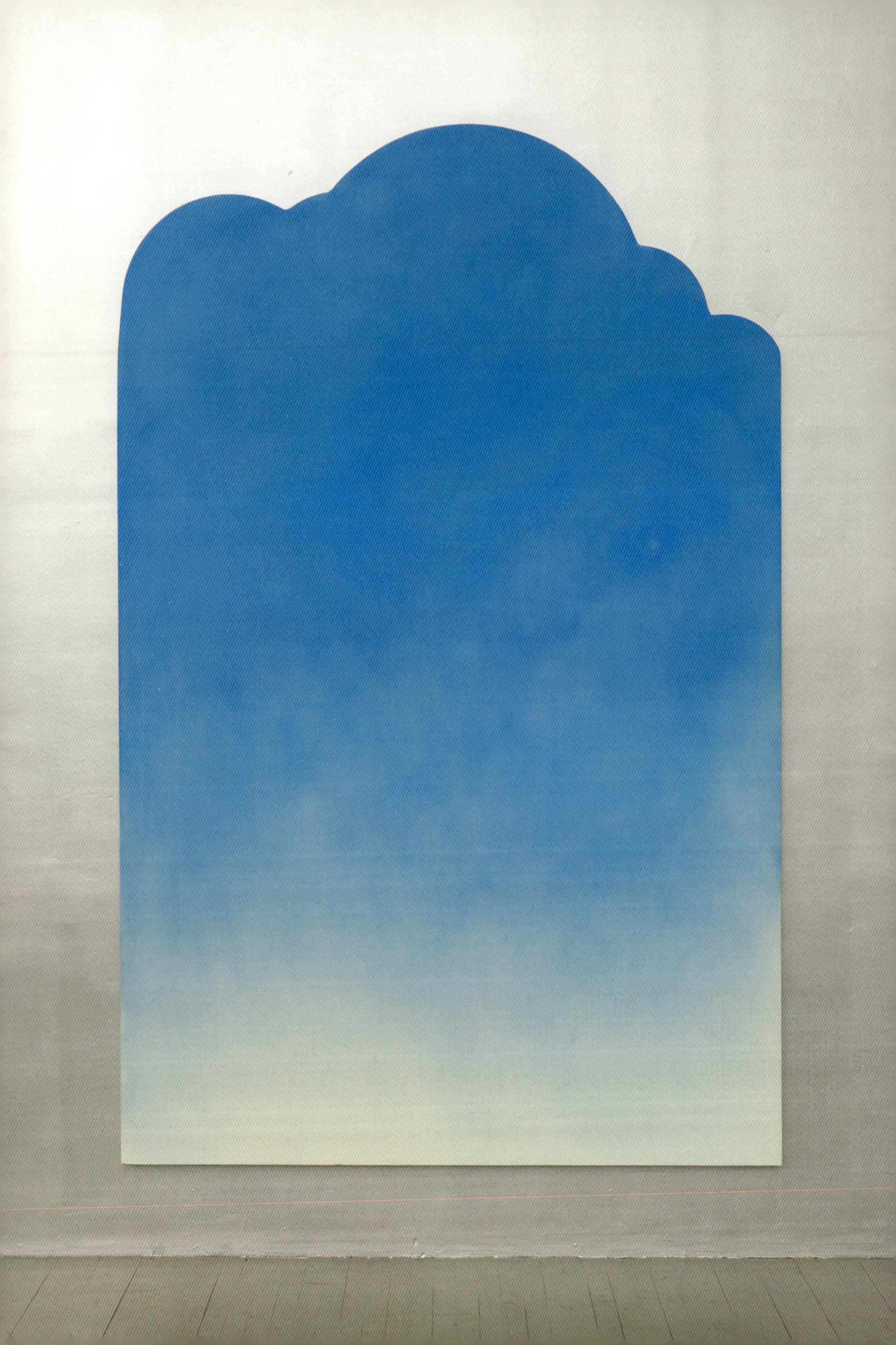

Other times the assemblages are even somewhat perverse, and
there are deliberate clashes, like those I set up between
Luginbühl and Ugo Rondinone's painting, which reminds me
of the Renaissance with its Fra Angelico sky. It's as if a
fresco has been extracted from a chapel and all of the figures have been erased. There is something in that blue sky
that speaks to magnificence, meditation, and fullness.
The shape of Rondinone's

> *achternovemberzweitausendundvierzehn*, 2014
> Acrylic on canvas, plexiglass plaque
> with caption
> 270 × 180 × 3 inches
> pp. 6, 20, 26, 29, 75

is very architectural, but also something of a stage set,
so I thought it would function perfectly as a theatrical
background, which is why we placed it in contrast to David
Hominal's

> *Animal with Baggage*, 2010
> Mixed media
> 8½ × 2½ × 4¾ inches
> pp. 28, 35

part of a collection of little sculptures made from found
objects. This crack pipe on a grape stem is joined by a
lighter, a bouquet made of mussel shells, and what looks like
a cocktail decoration with a little skull and a clothespin,
all placed on pedestals made from tin cans. There is something very grim about Hominal's objects—they are very hard
and gritty. I'm not sure how to say it: I feel like they
are desperate assemblages, a construction of things, yet
I'm unsure what they're meant to signify. Usually, each one
is presented on a different plinth, but I wanted to create a
single platform for all of them.

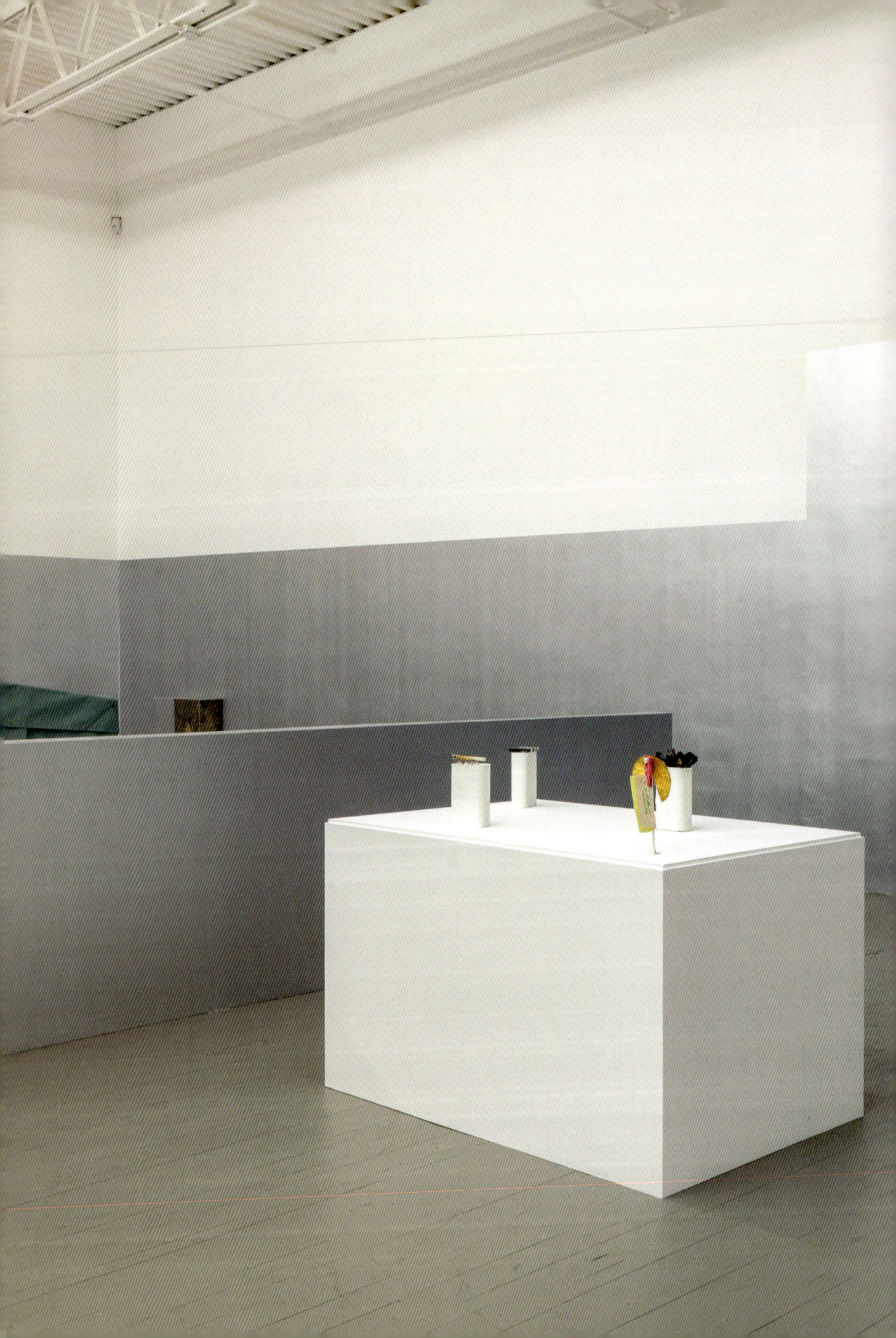

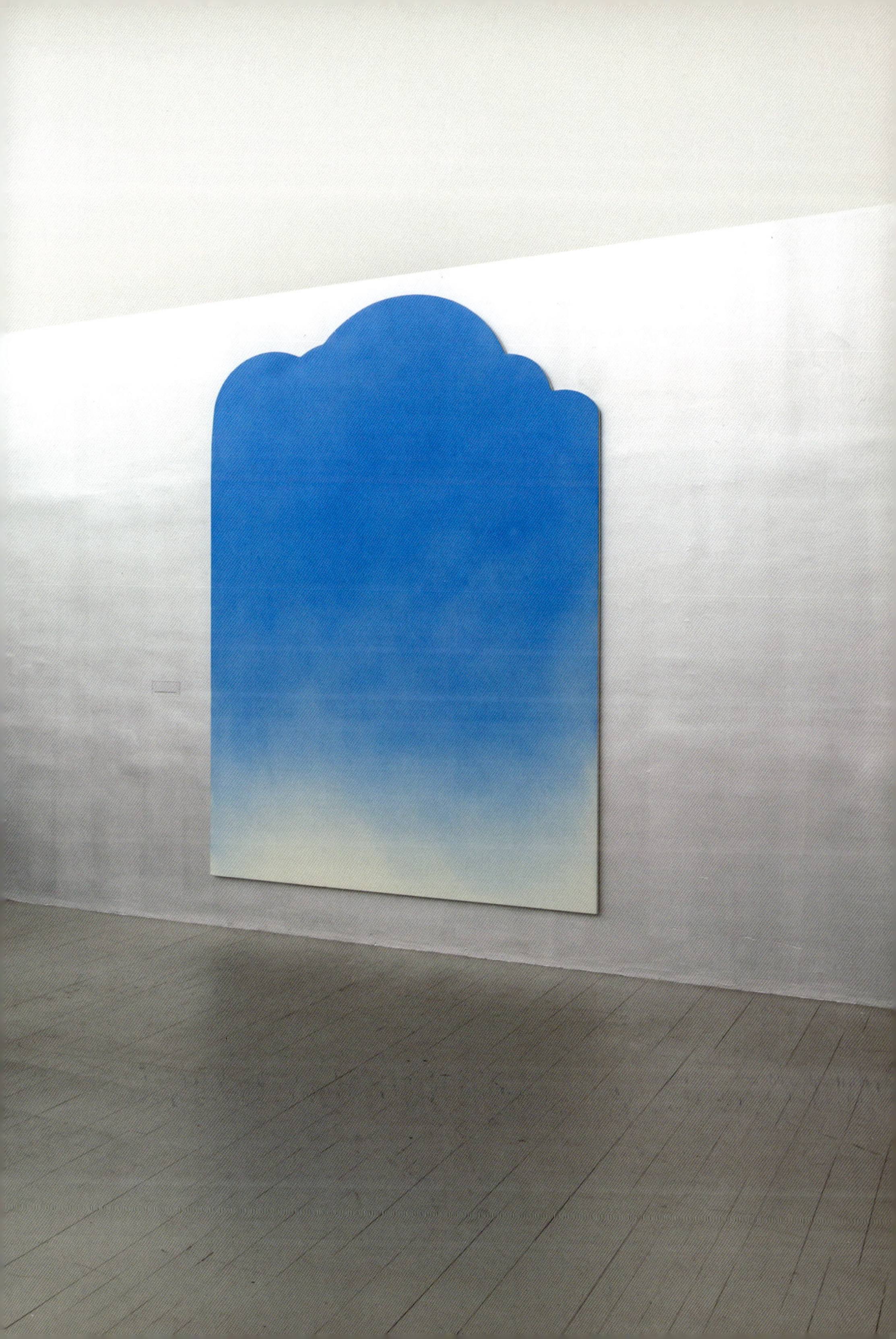

David Hominal
pp. 20, 28, 31: *Ni le soleil ni la mort*, 2011
pp. 20, 28, 33: *ST070910-II*, 2010
pp. 28, 34: *ST070910*, 2010

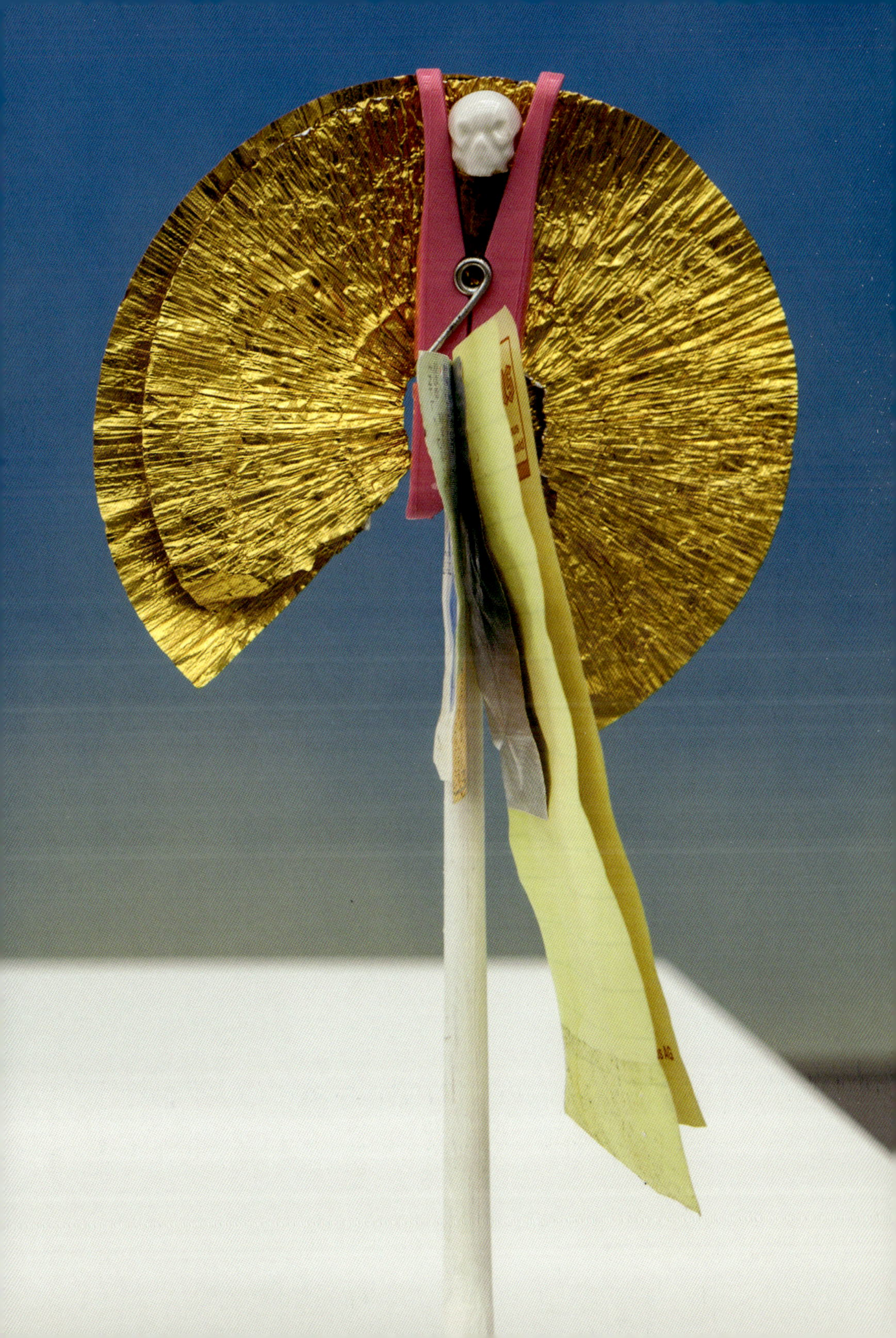

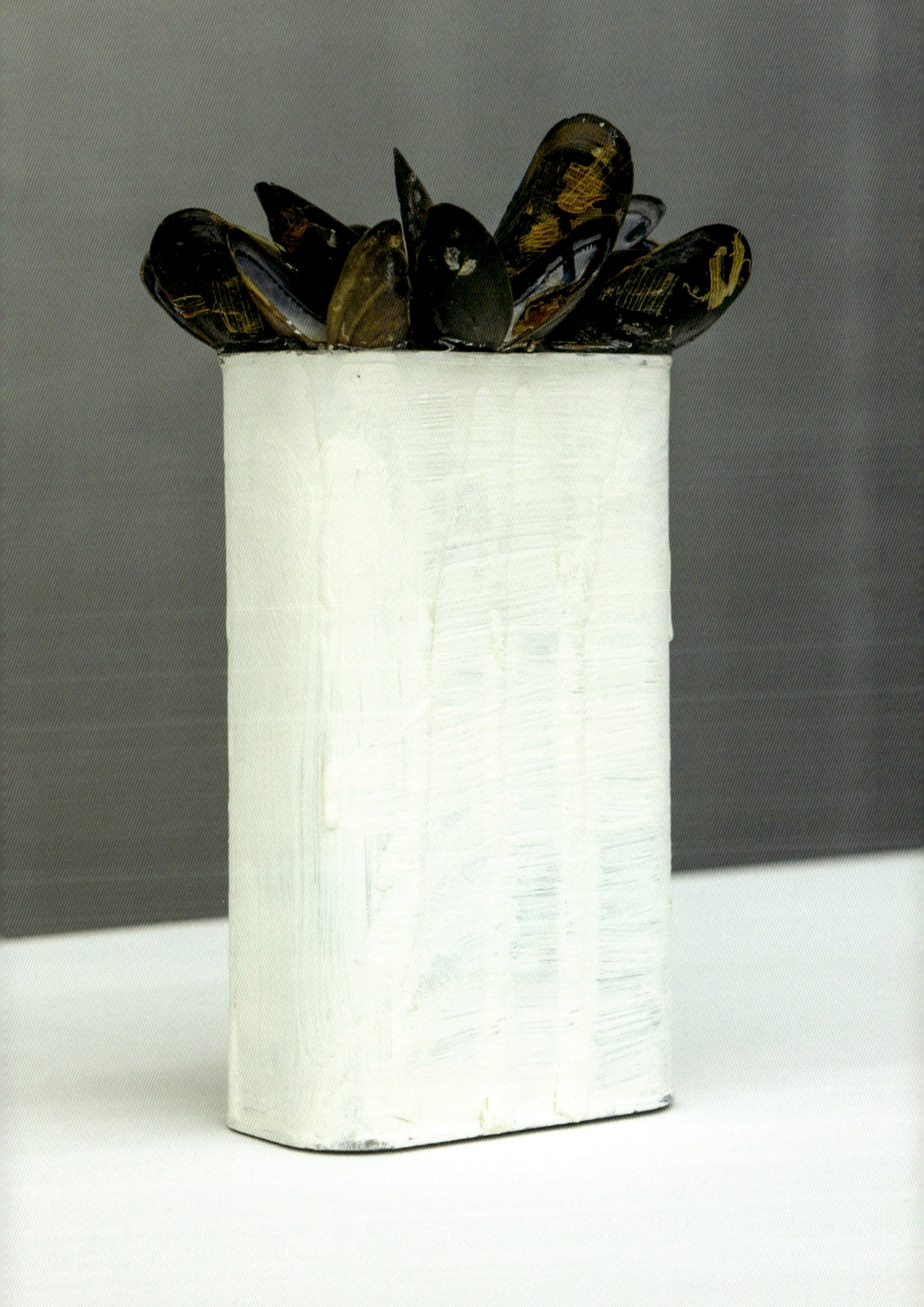

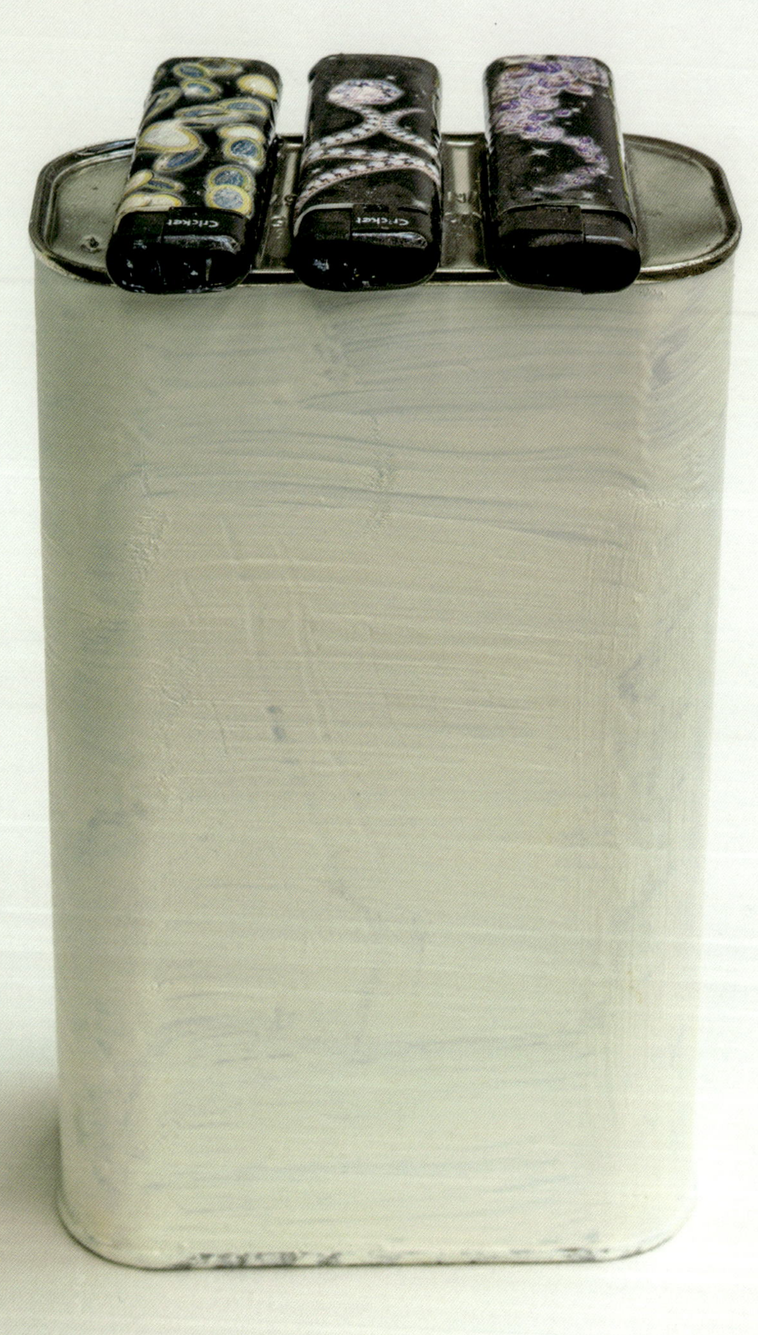

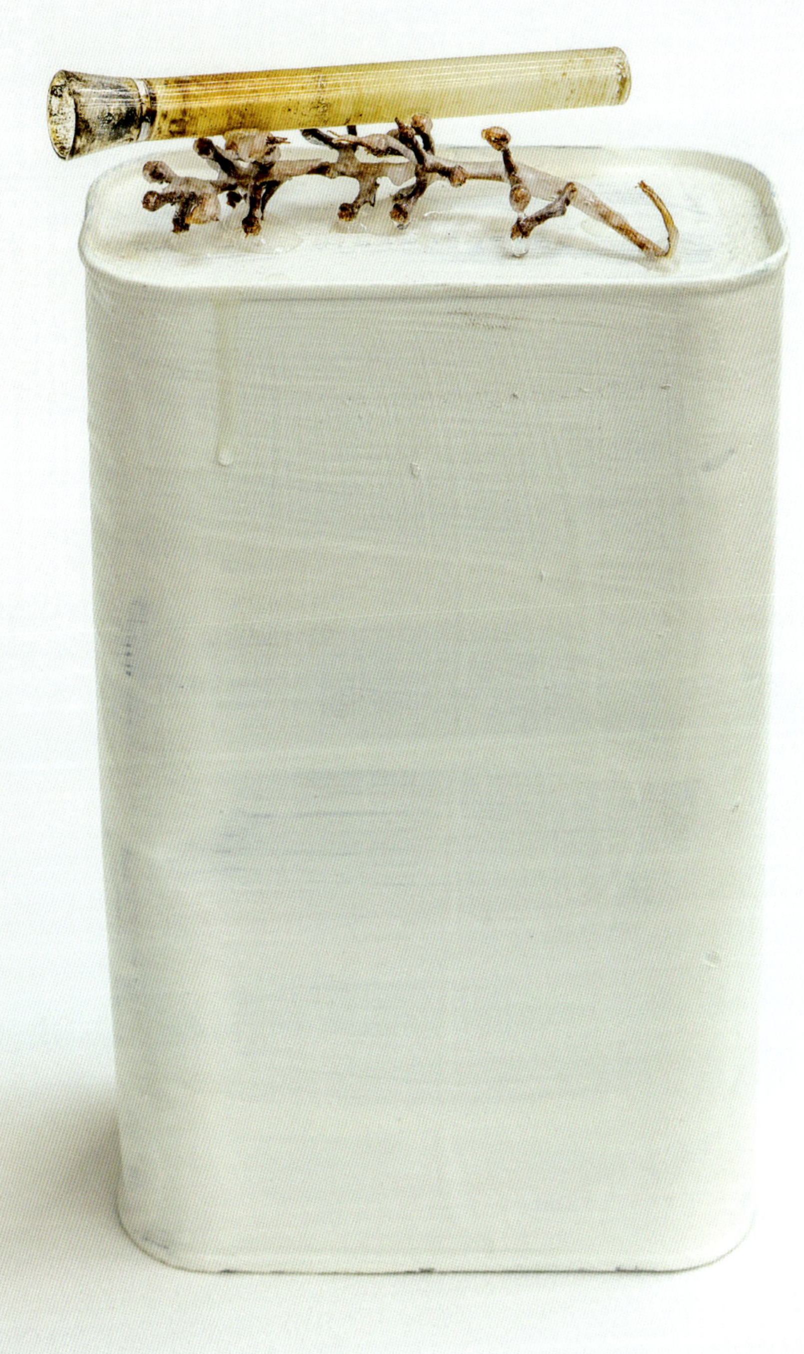

There are some connections that simply worked out, like the one
between the Rondinone and Mathis Gasser's painting, which is
a political statement of sorts. I have a fascination with geo-
politics. Not a monstrous obsession, but I like to be aware of
what is happening. In this work, it's as if the map of Europe
is suddenly being held together by metal beams. The first line—
an allegorical line referred to as *la banane bleue*—goes all
the way from northwest England to southern Italy, which is the
most densely populated and economically active zone in Europe,
with a high concentration of wealth. This zone is similar to
the Rust Belt in the United States, which includes industrial
cities like Detroit that have now fallen on hard times. I didn't
speak to Gasser about his painting

Superstructures for Europe, 2012
Acrylic on canvas
14 × 10 inches
pp. 25, 37, 39

but, for me, it's a kind of geopolitical-mapping approach to
painting. Because it's atmospheric and very light, you get a
sense of something muddy, as if the lines of Europe have been
rubbed out and everything is held together with the force of
the superstructure.

pp. 38, 73: Fabian Marti, *Amber and Green Egg with 10 Breeding Ouroboroi*, 2014

pp. 39, 73, 82: Méret Oppenheim, *Traccia Table*, 1972

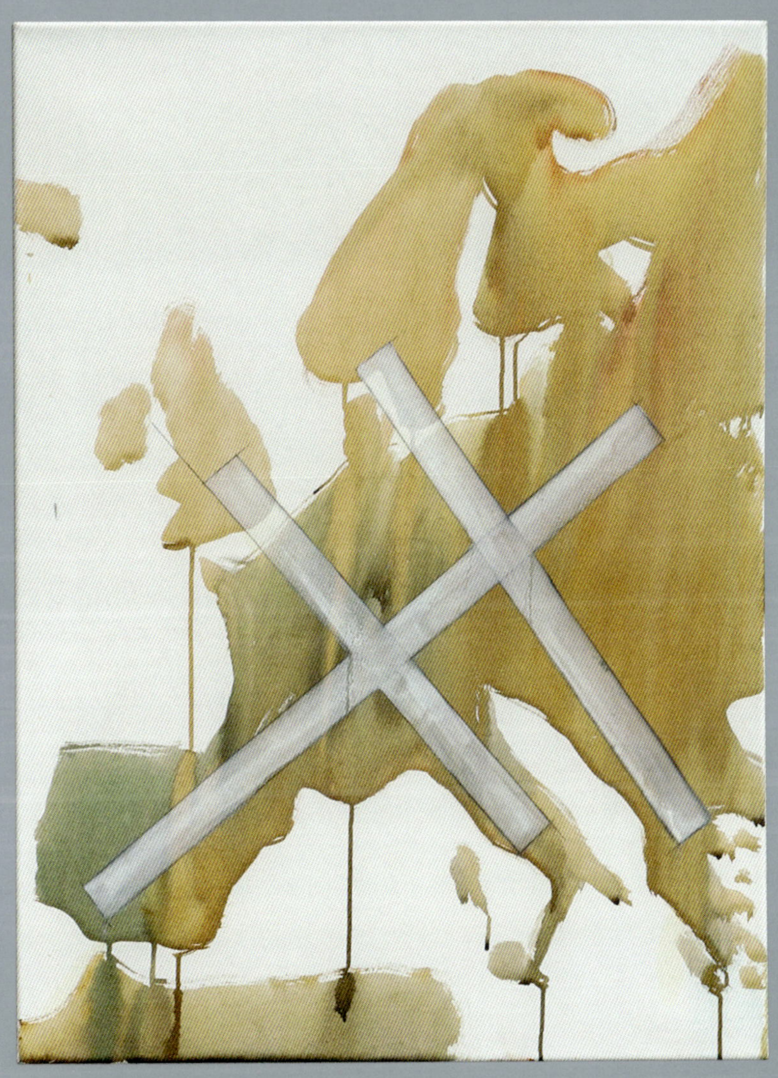

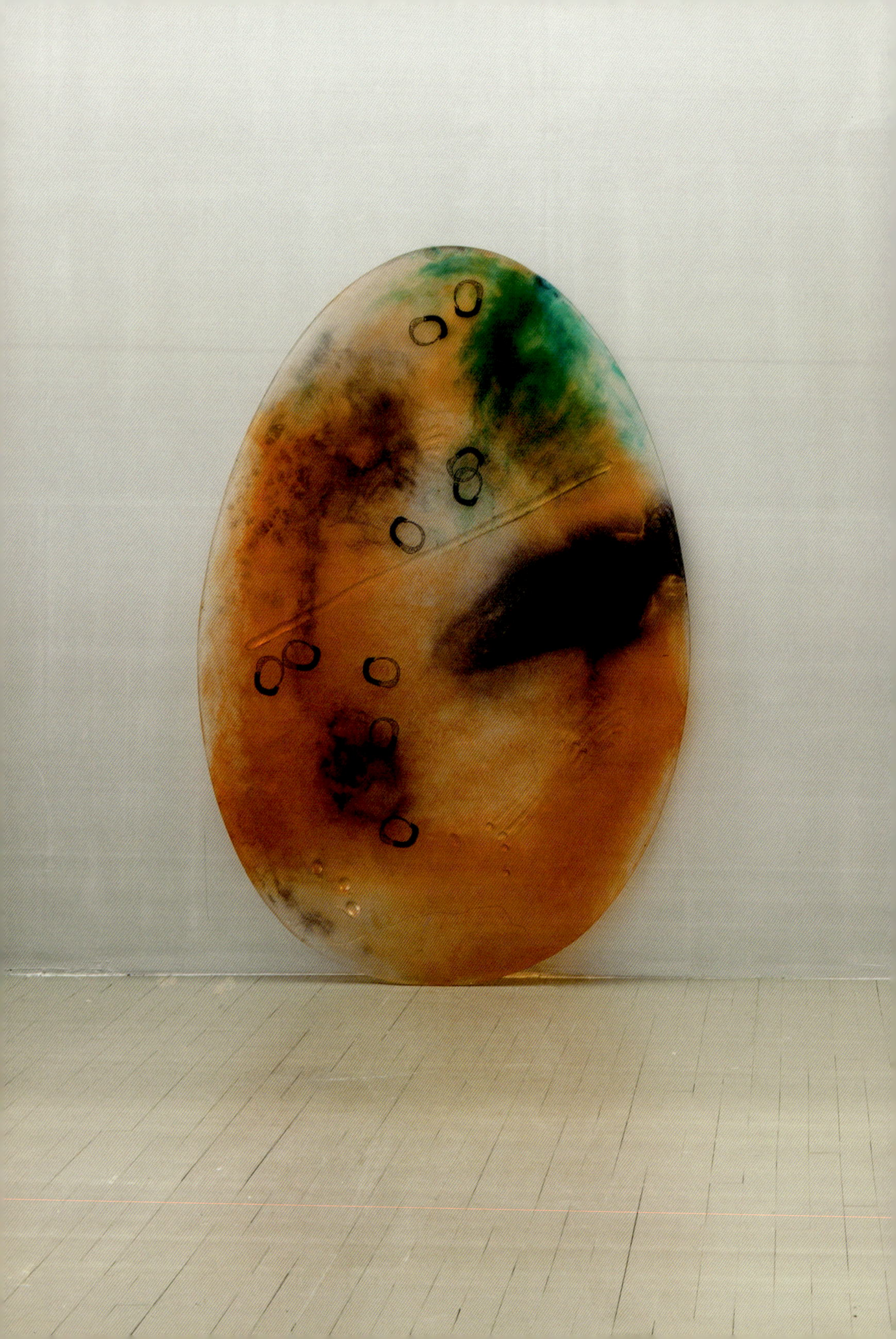

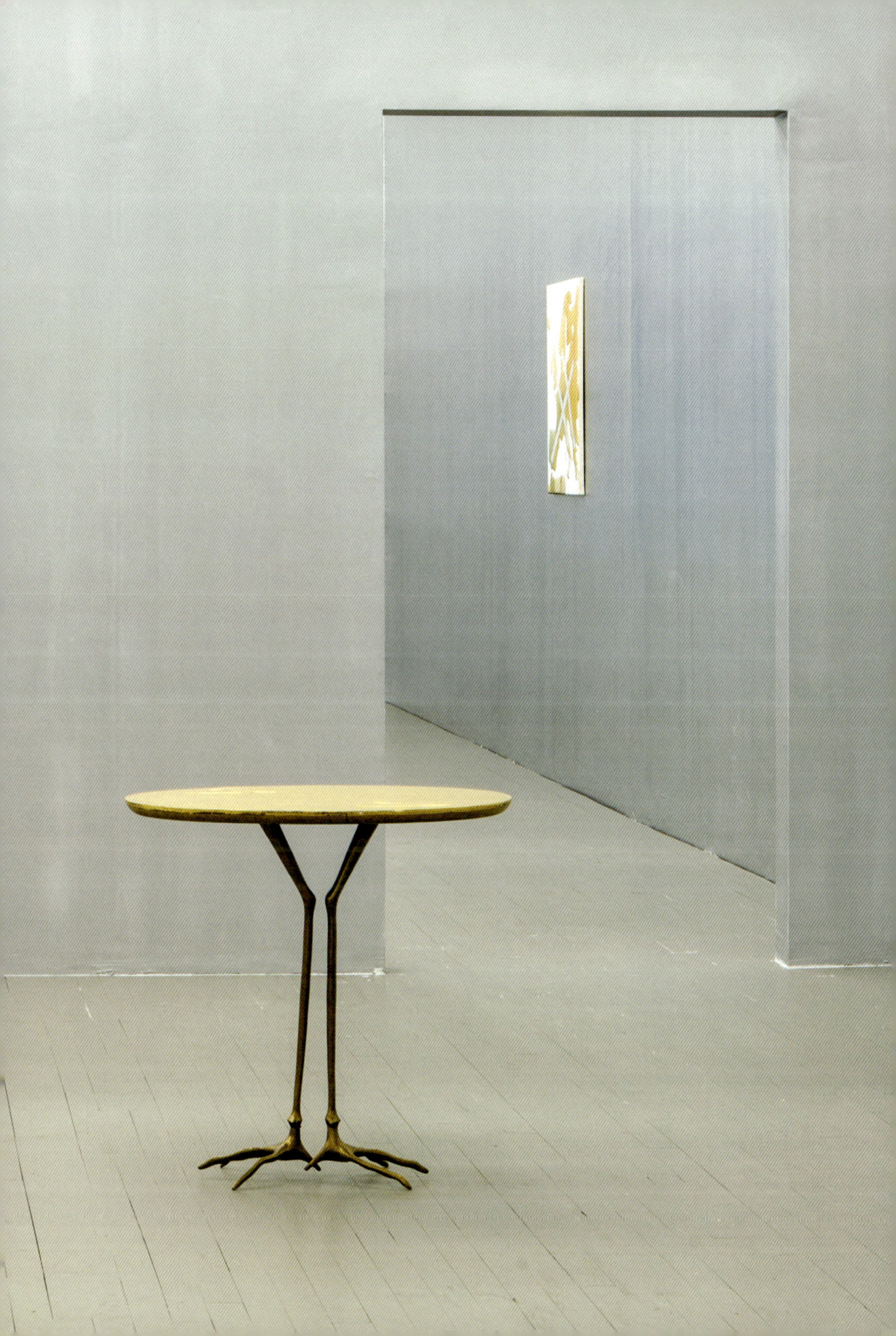

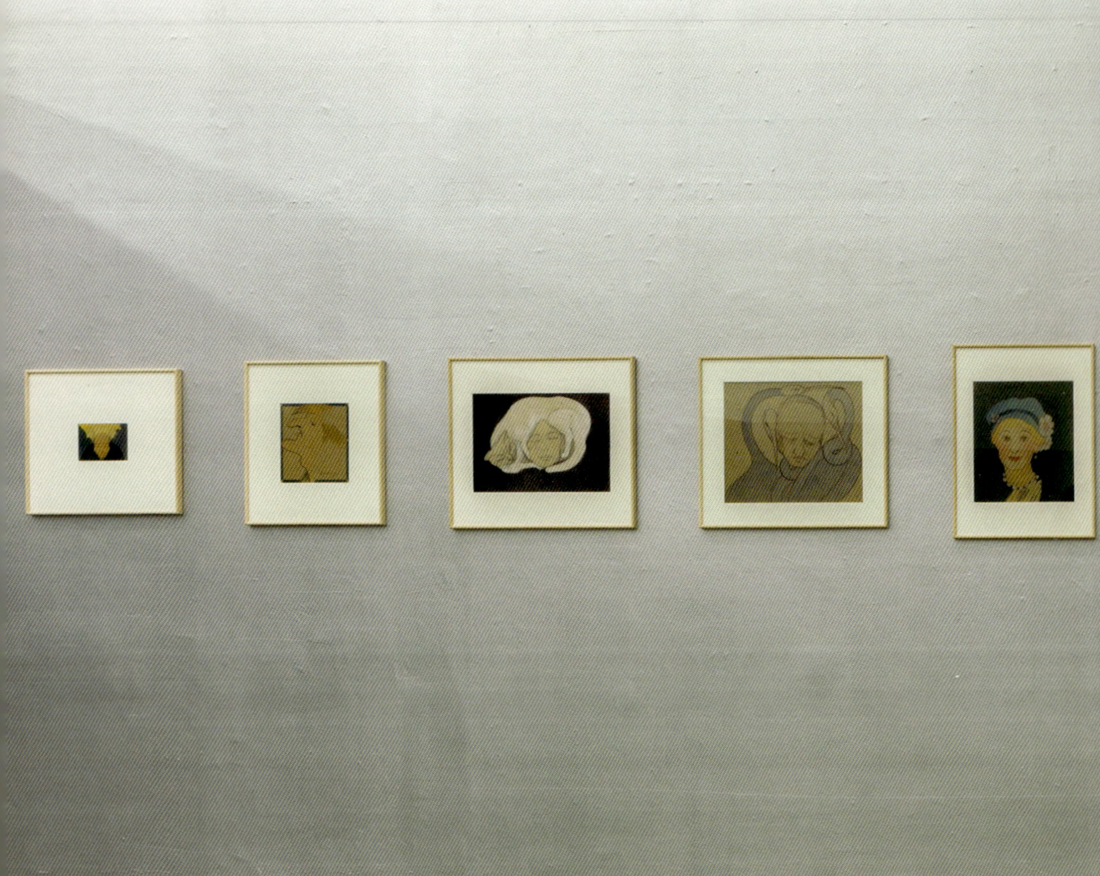

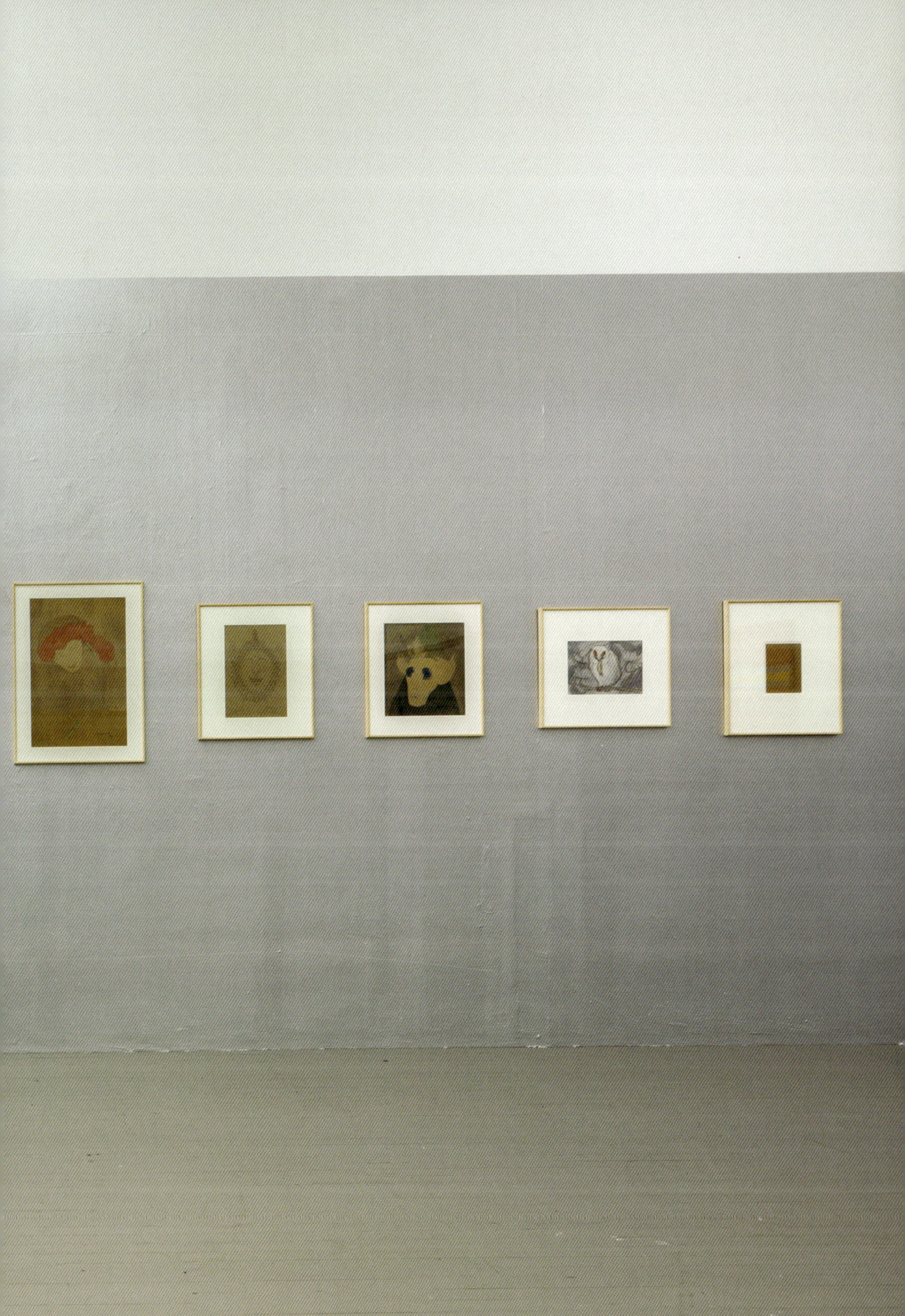

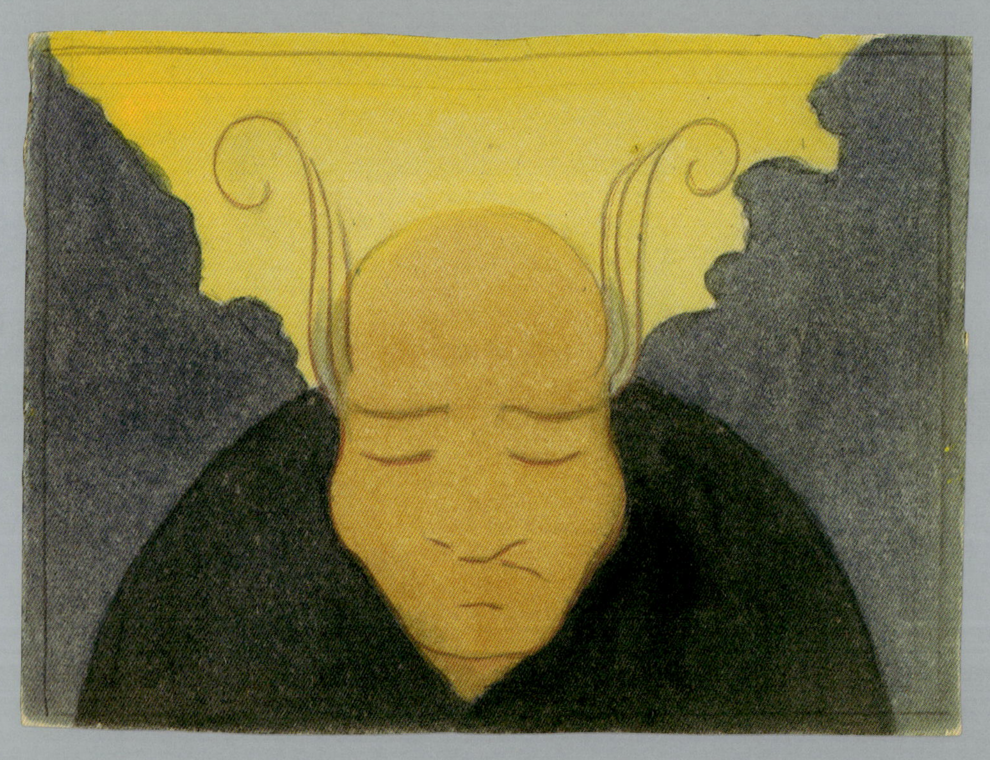

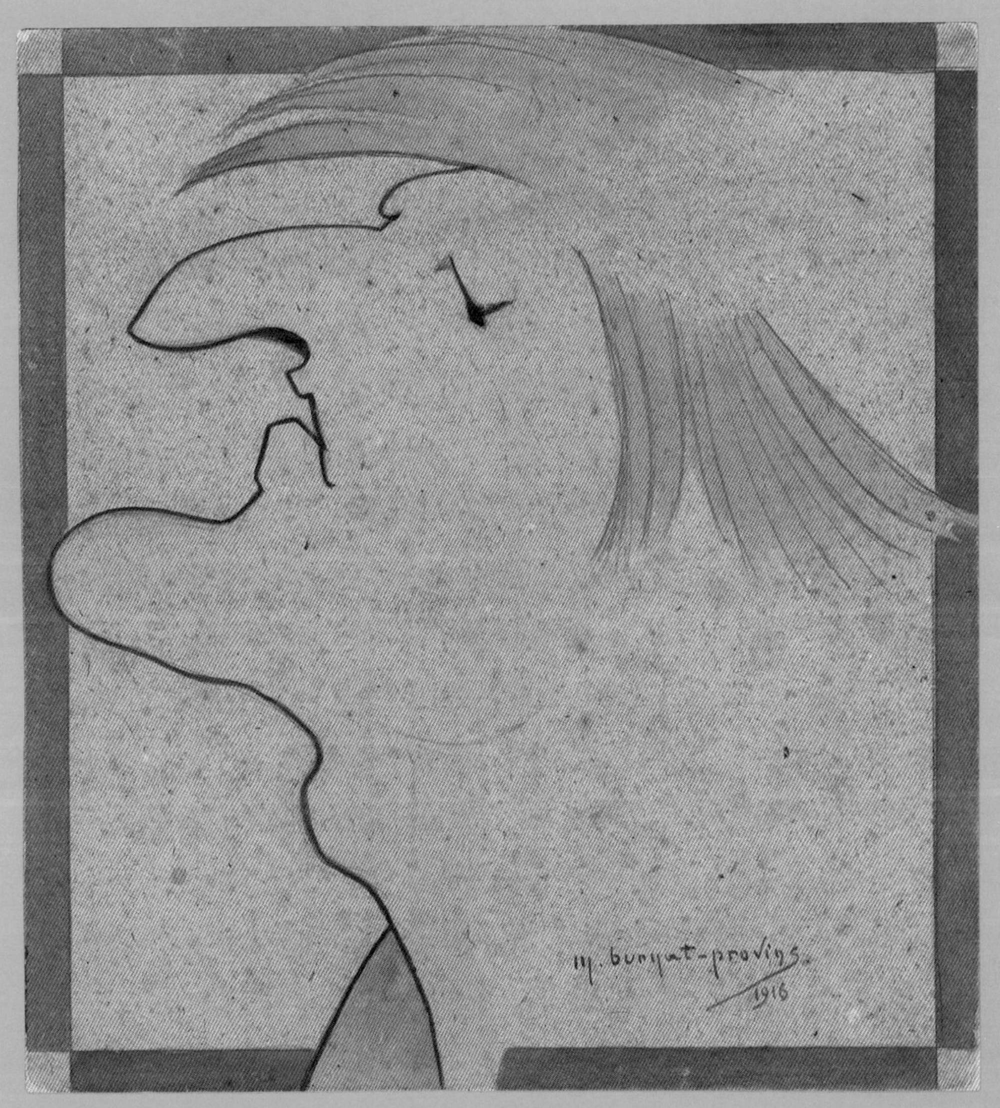

M. burnat-provins.
1916

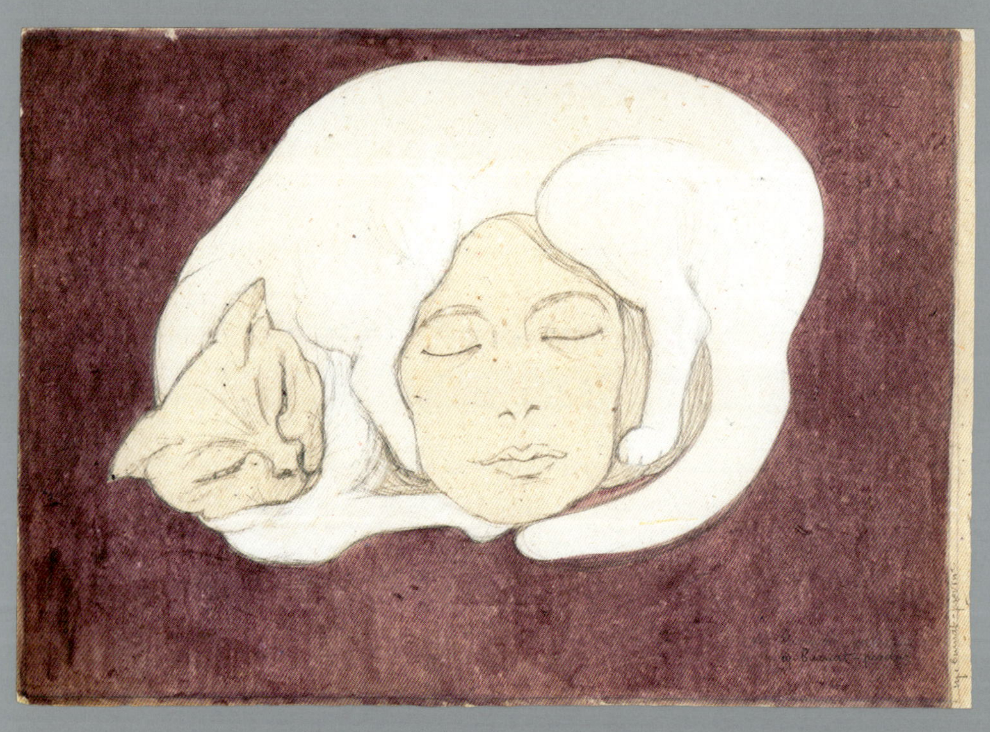

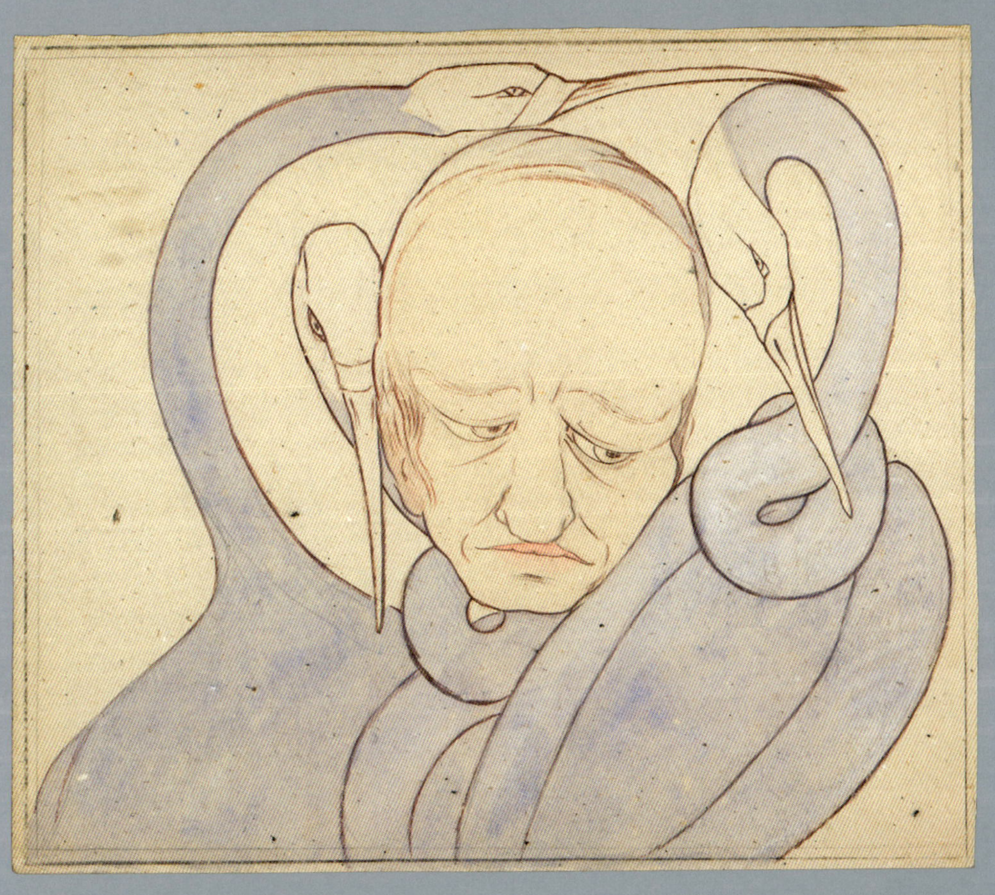

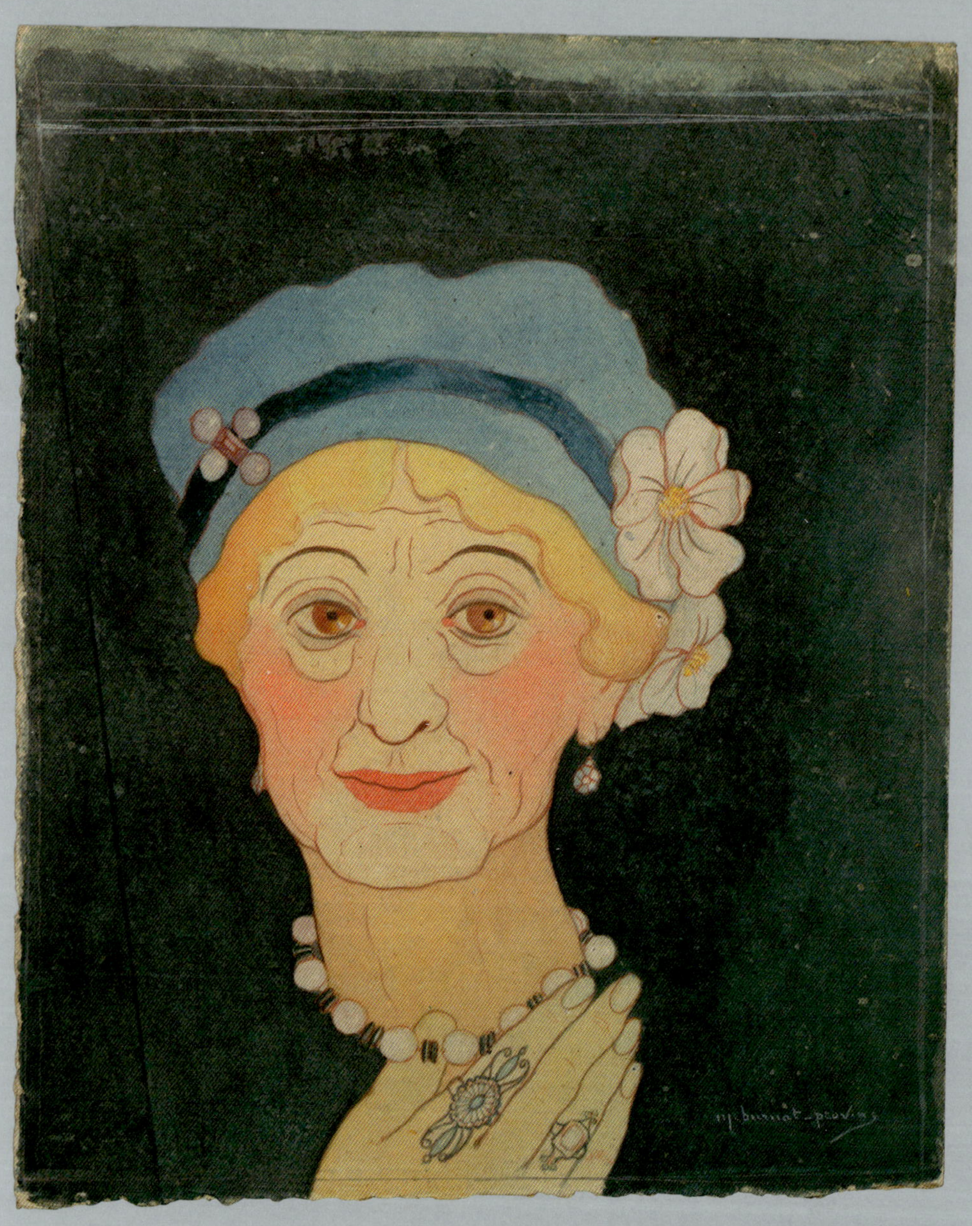
m. burnat-provins

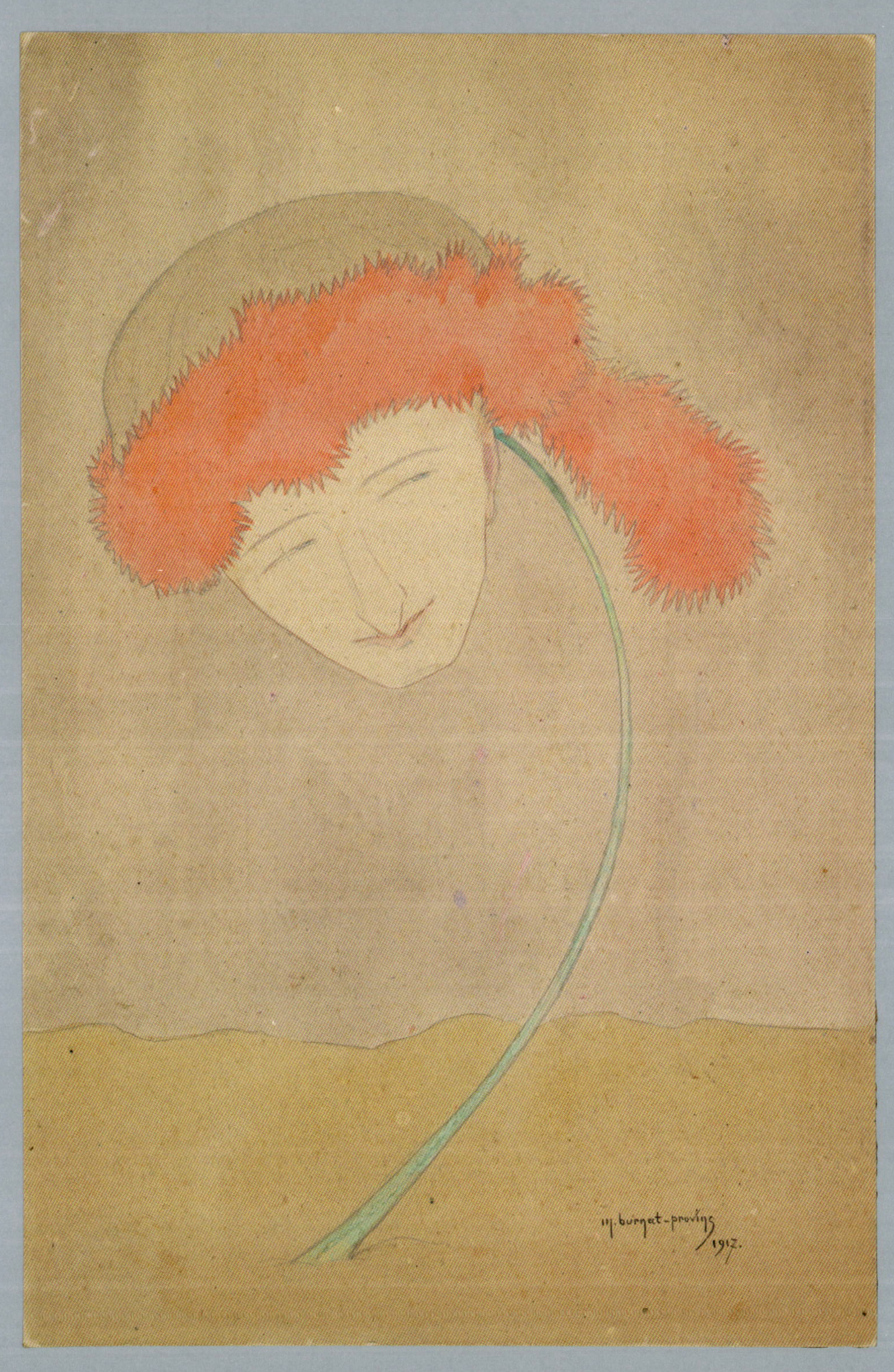
M. burnat-provins
1917.

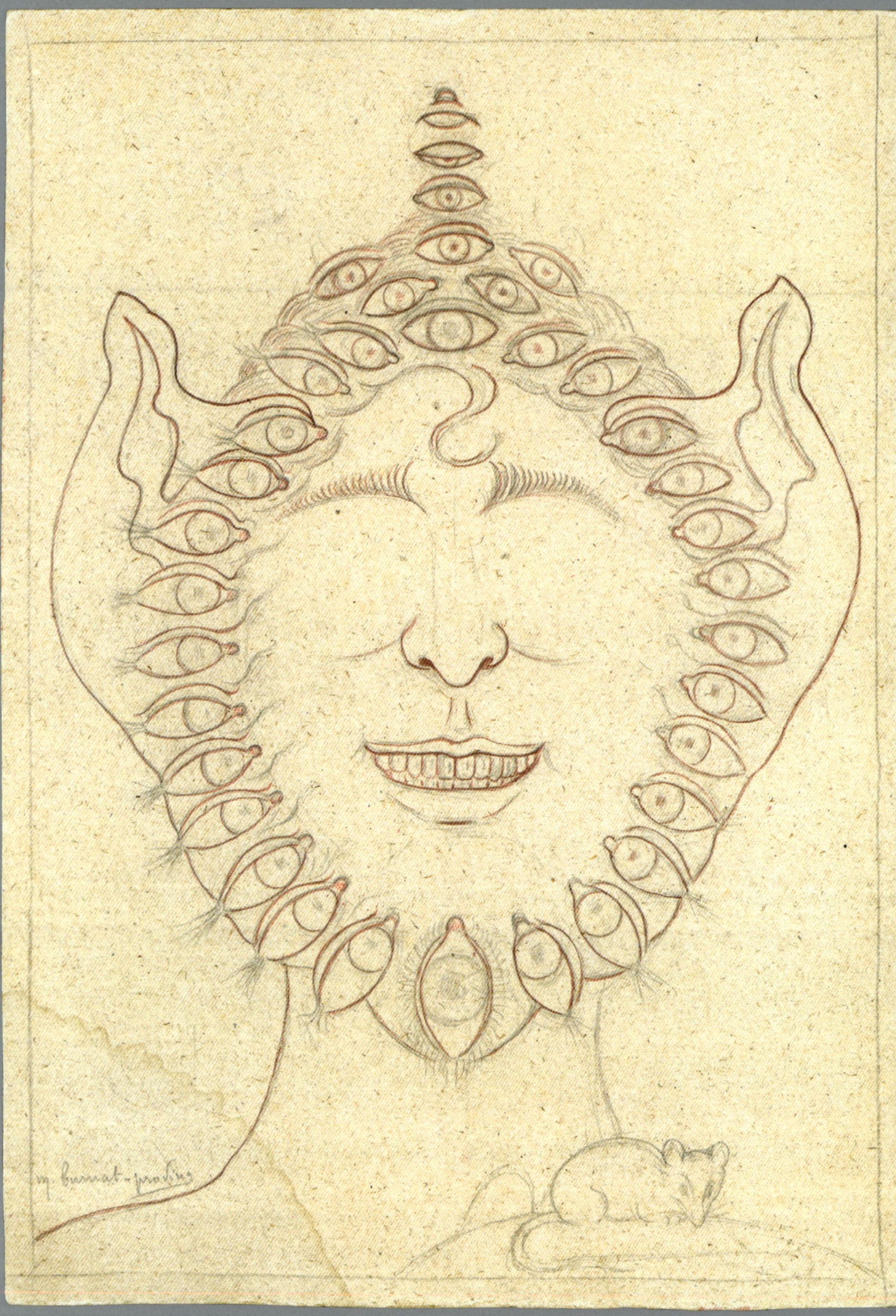

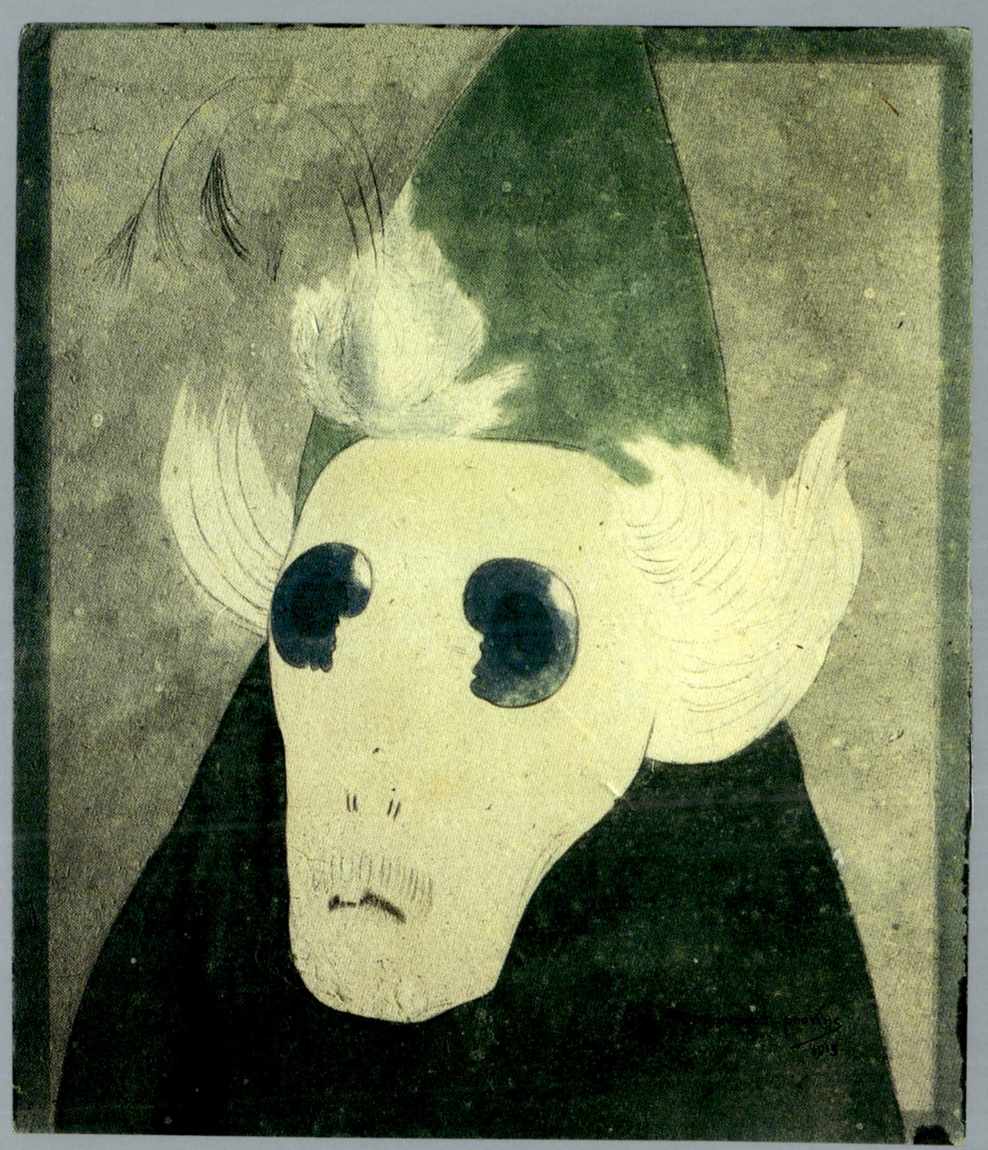

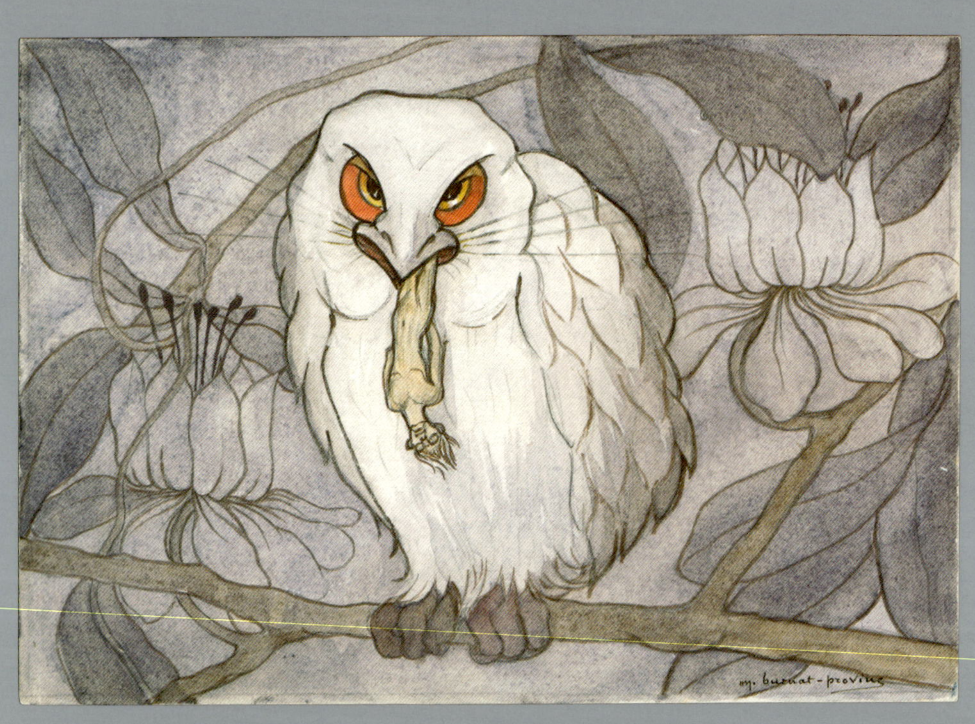

m. burnat-provins

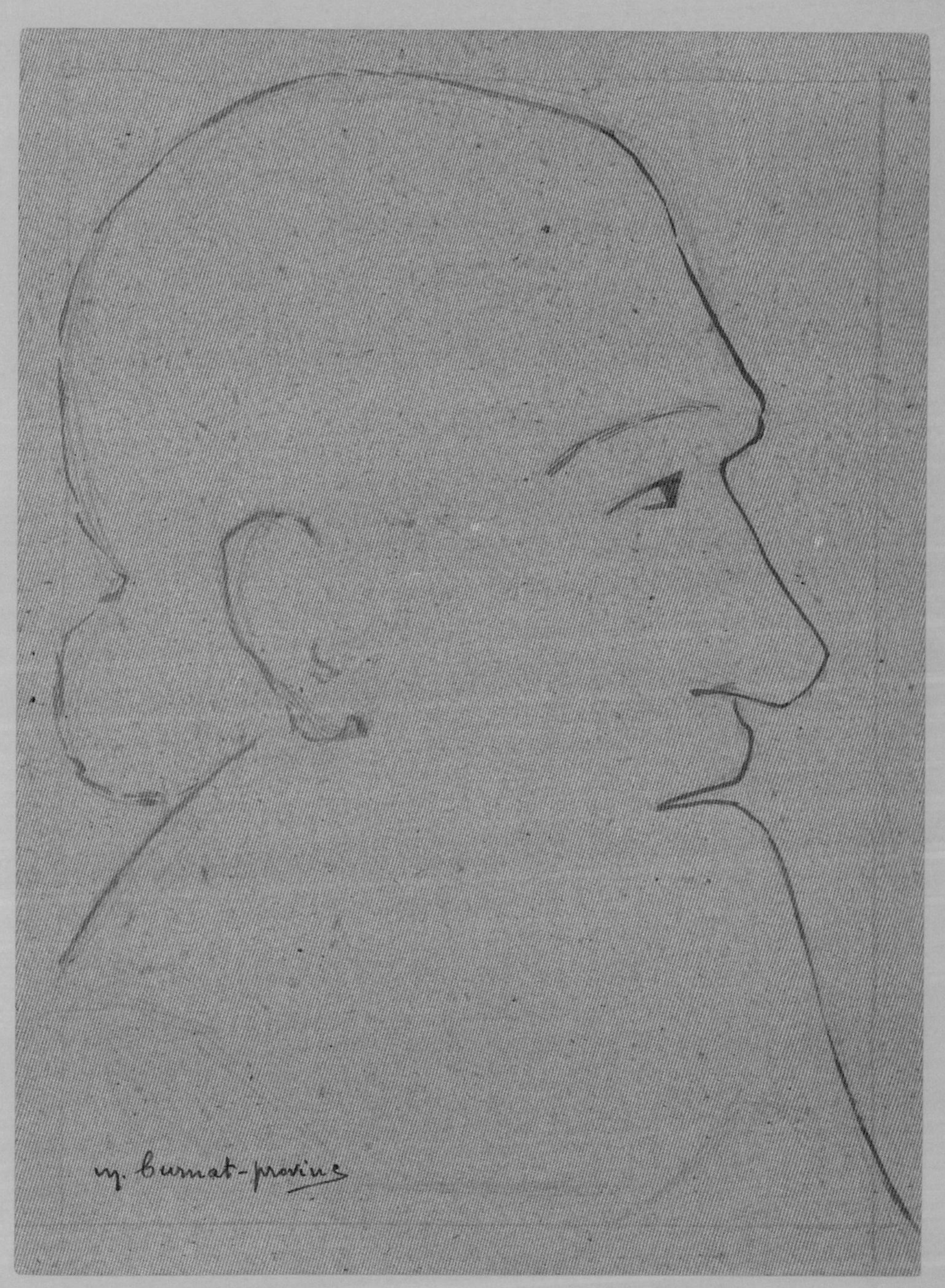
m. burnat-provins

Then there is Sylvain Croci-Torti's work, which was familiar
to me because it throws itself desperately into extreme ref-
erentiality in an effort to be part of the lineage of art
history. There's an obstinacy, a fury, and at the same time
a profound eagerness by the artist to participate in established forms. I appreciate the completely formal aspects of
Croci-Torti's

Lost in Confusion, 2014
Acrylic on canvas
47¼ × 59¼ inches
pp. 25, 53

I found the monochrome blue quite beautiful. The surface is
divided into three parts and painted using a silk-screening
squeegee. We installed this painting in the same room as the
Luginbühl. I thought this pairing was strange and funny and
relevant to Hominal's little pieces behind them. Even if these
artists are forty years or more apart, and the materials and
dimensions of their respective works are different, all have
a similar intention. They share this idea of collaging and
assembling disparate materials.

Marguerite Burnat-Provins

pp. 40, 42: *Cenio L'abruti!*, 1934

pp. 40, 43, 108: *Croix le désagréable*, 1916

pp. 40, 44, 82: *Hanugre et le chat*, 1919

pp. 40, 45, 82: *Asclibour entoure*, 1929

pp. 40, 46, 82: *Coquetterie*, 1932

pp. 41, 47, 82: *La tête qui se balance*, 1917

pp. 41, 48, 82: *La curiosité*, 1935

pp. 41, 49, 82: *Frilute le peureux*, 1915

pp. 41, 50, 82: *La vie est-ce bon?*, undated

pp. 41, 51, 82: *Mauglu Professeur*, 1918

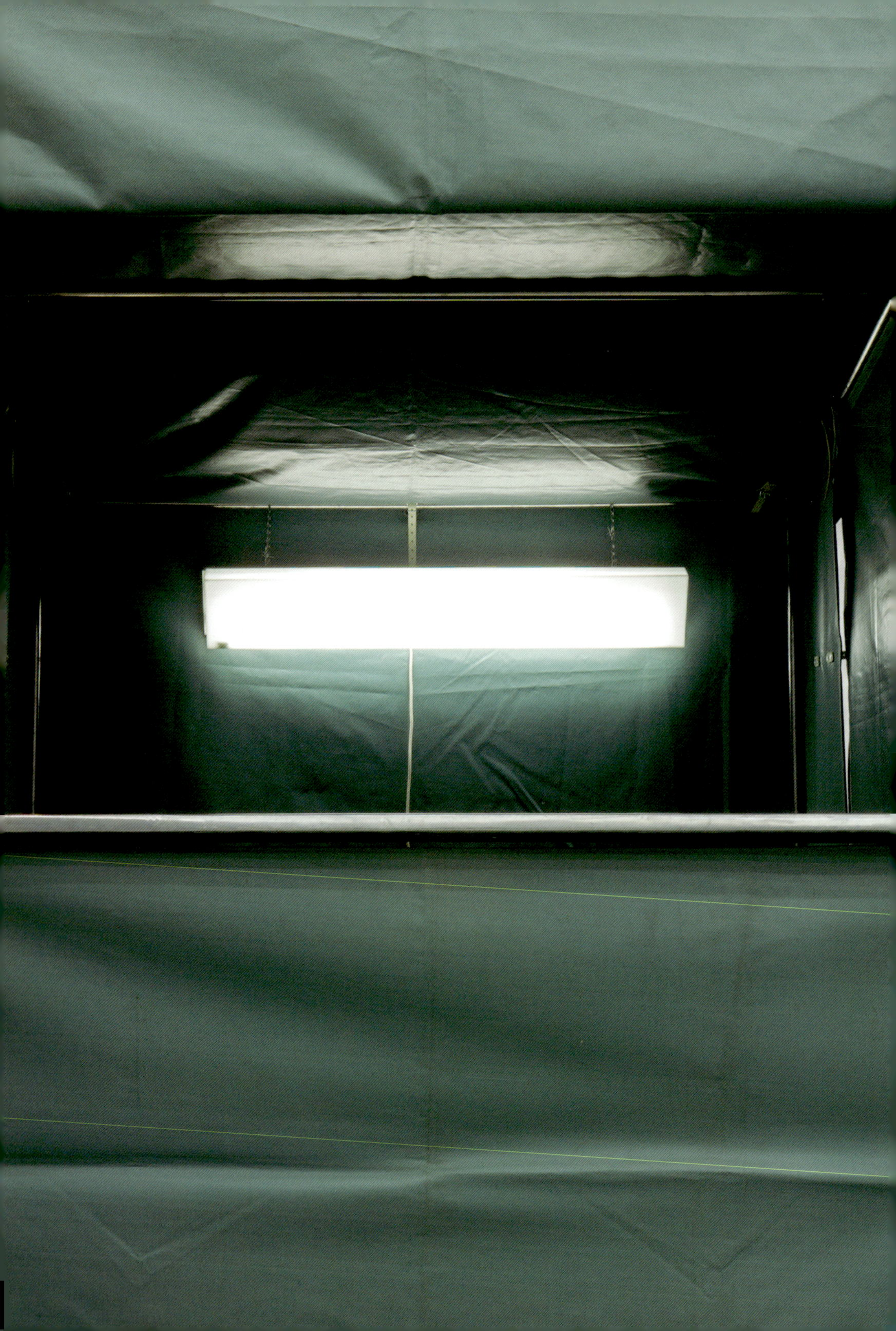

I first encountered Fabrice Gygi when I was about twenty years old and I had really gotten into the minimalists. I have always had a fascination with

> *Tente-Bar*, 1997
> Metal, wood, tarpaulin, leather, neon,
> and plexiglass
> 98½ × 78¾ × 78¾ inches
> pp. 54, 74-75

The tent is the kind you find in a market or a public place during festivals. Gygi was one of my teachers and part of a whole generation of artists for whom minimalism stopped being enough. He comes from the generation of urban squatters who believed in reappropriating the means and materials of production. He once told me, "If society creates a tent that is standard and the dimensions are set, then I'll build my own tent." This work is both minimal and sculptural. It has a design sensibility with social implications that can be activated, and at the same time it can just be observed. I like that ambivalence.

pp. 56-65: Urs Lüthi, *Some day when my longing is gone, I'm gonna take a smile for a walk in the sun*, 1975

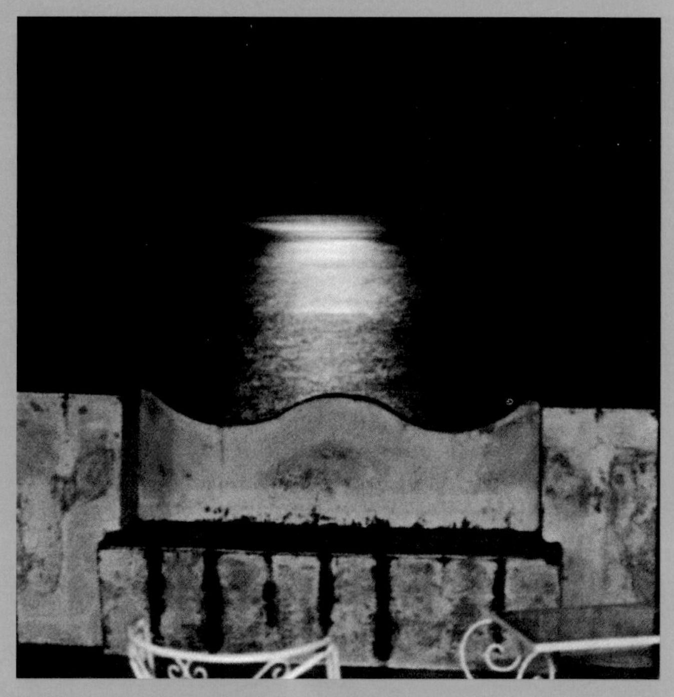

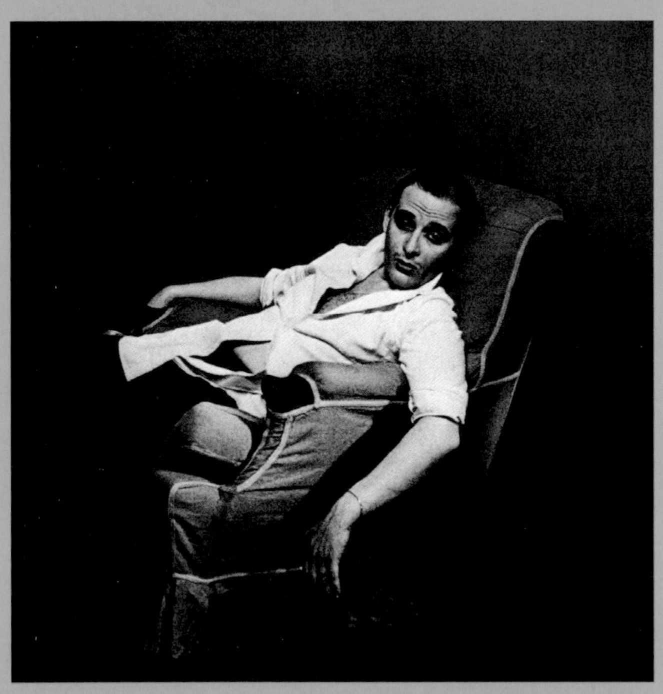

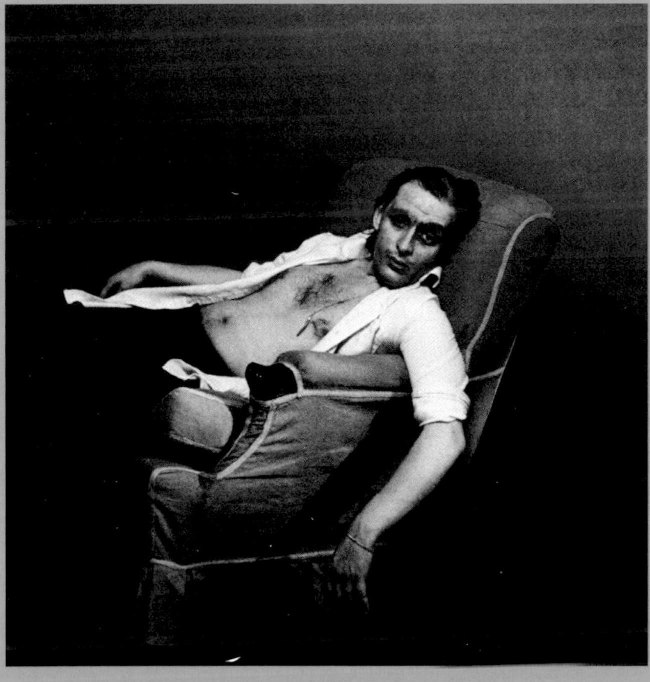

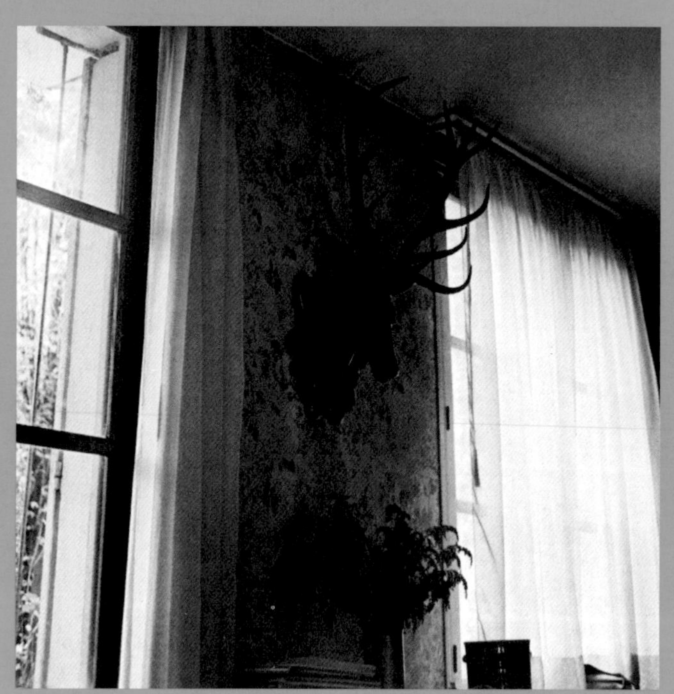

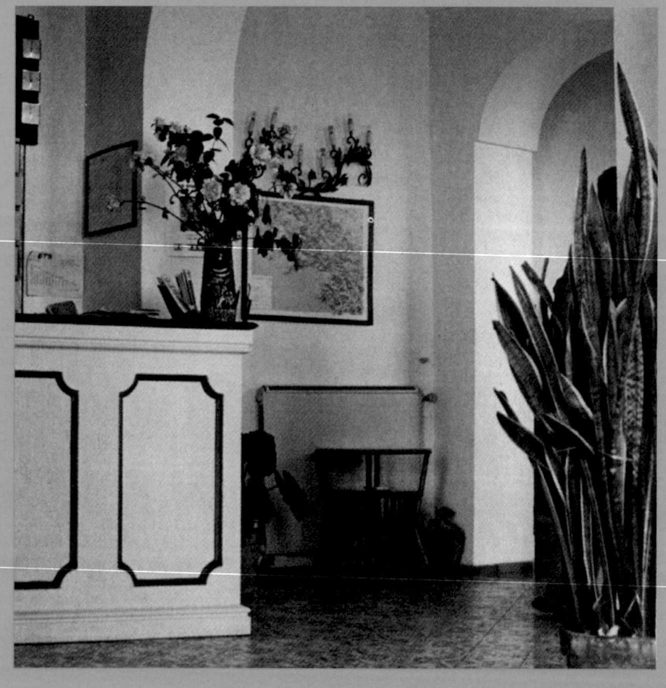

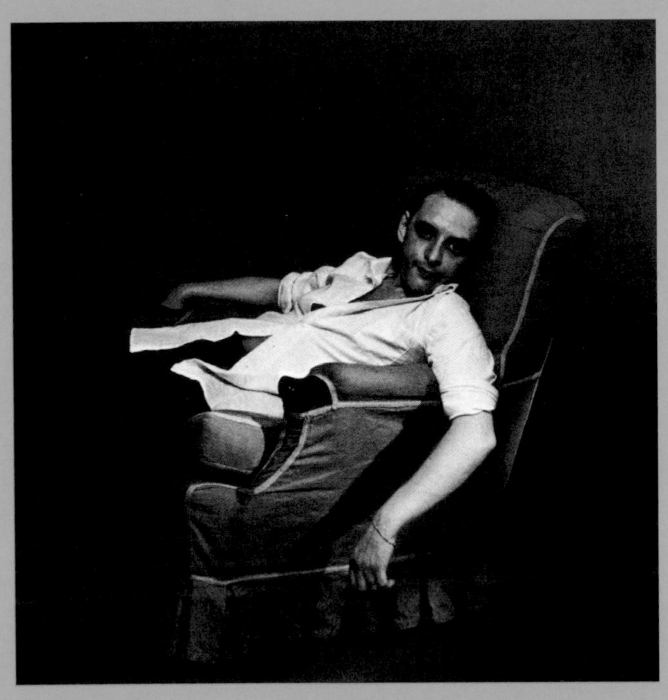

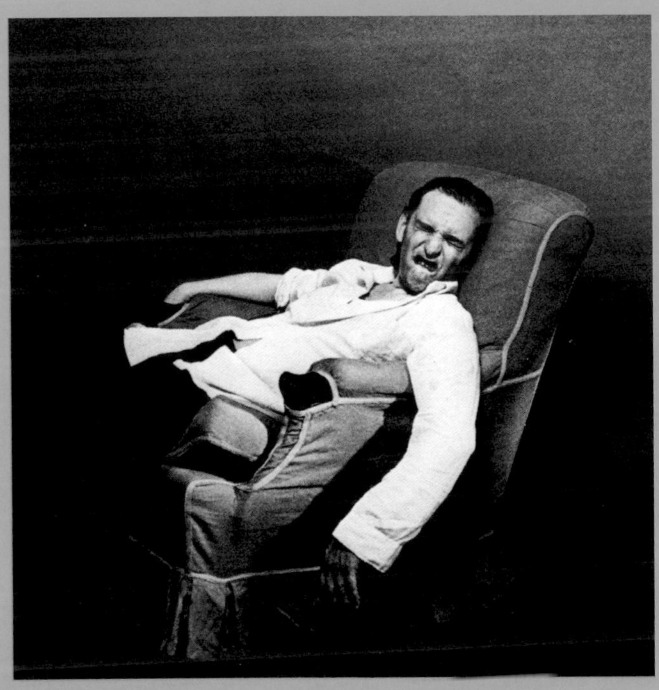

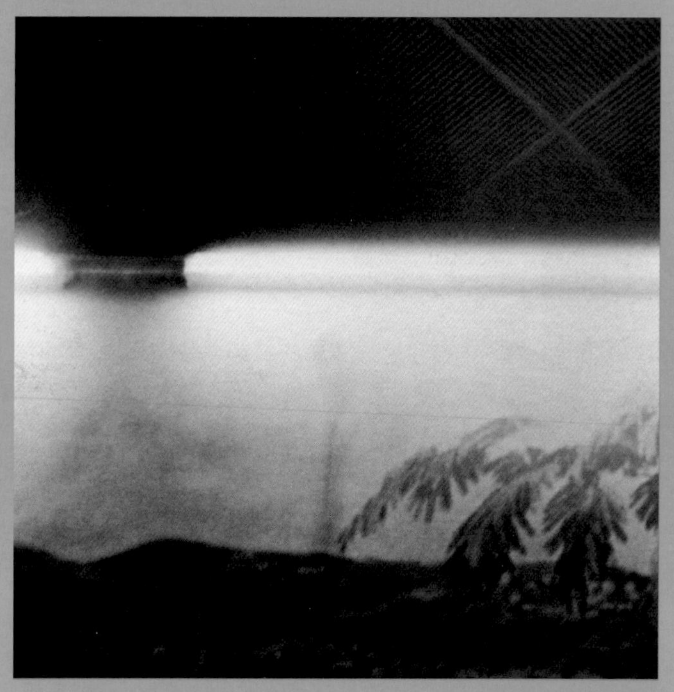

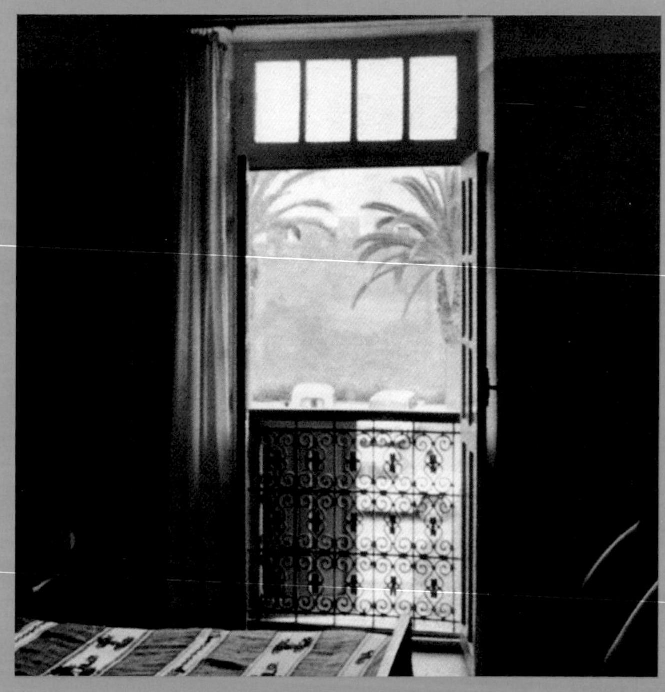

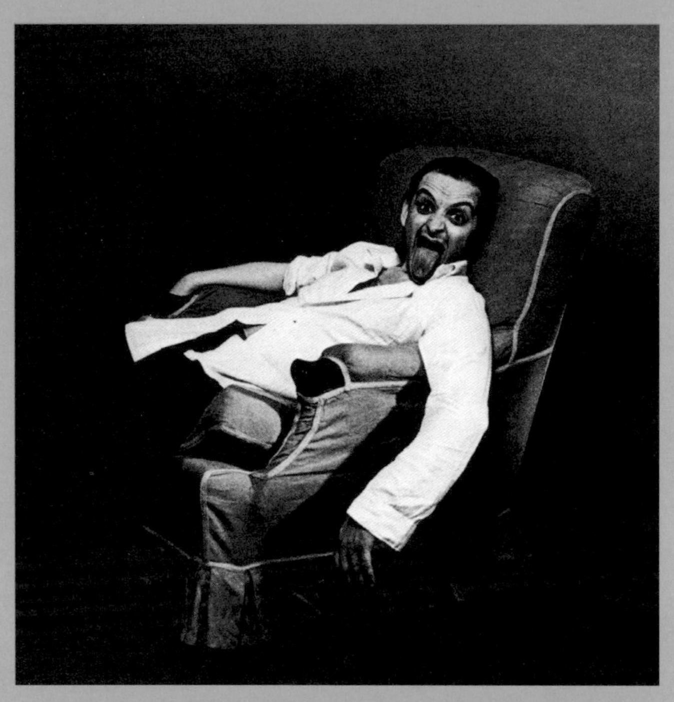

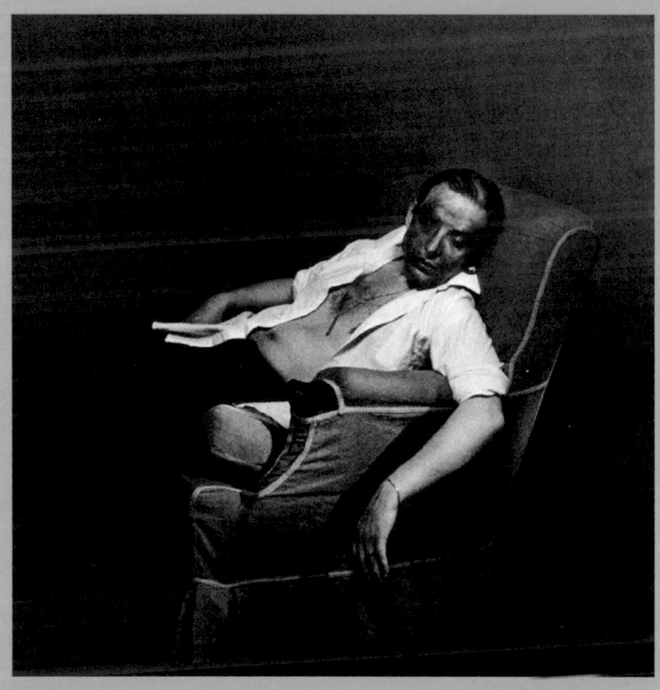

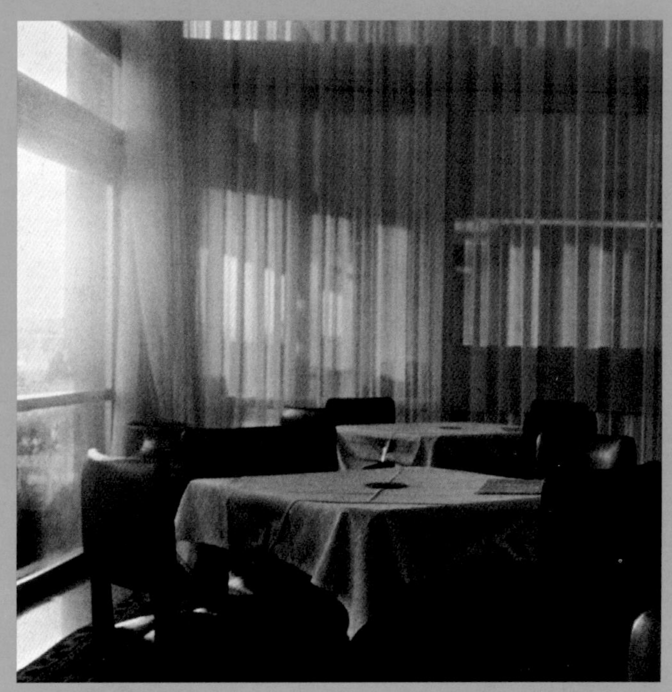

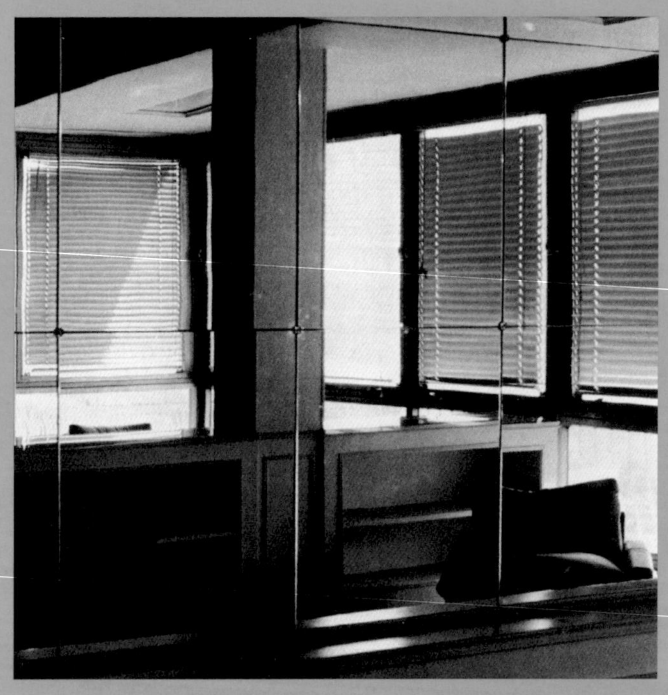

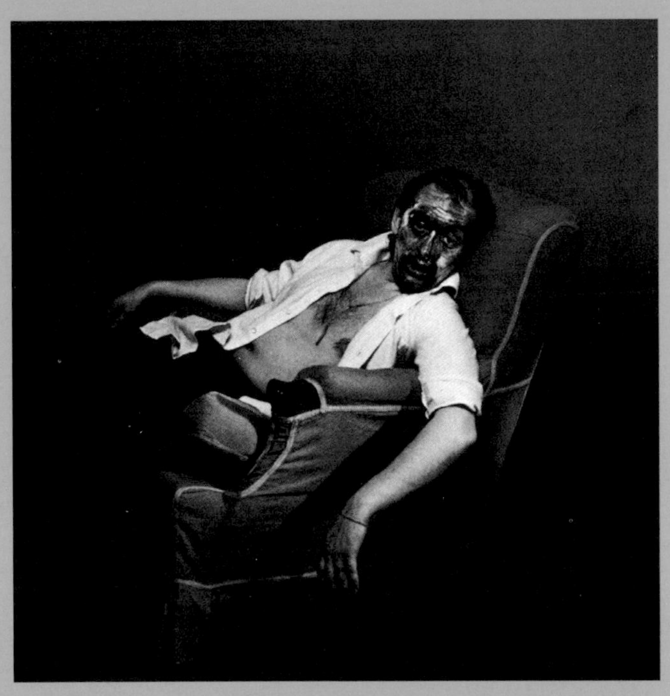

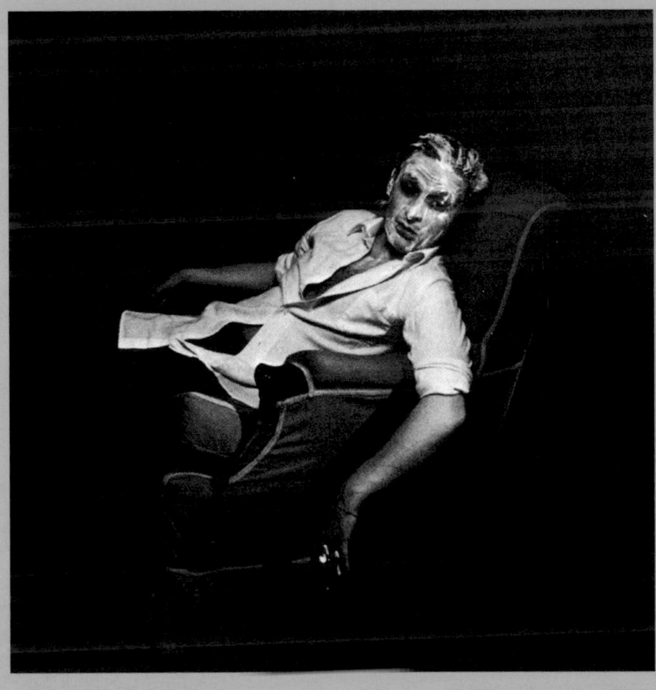

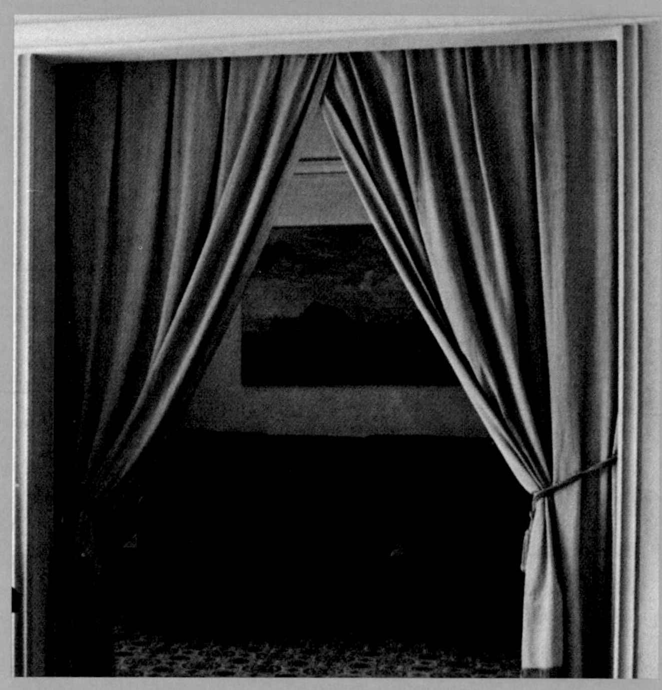

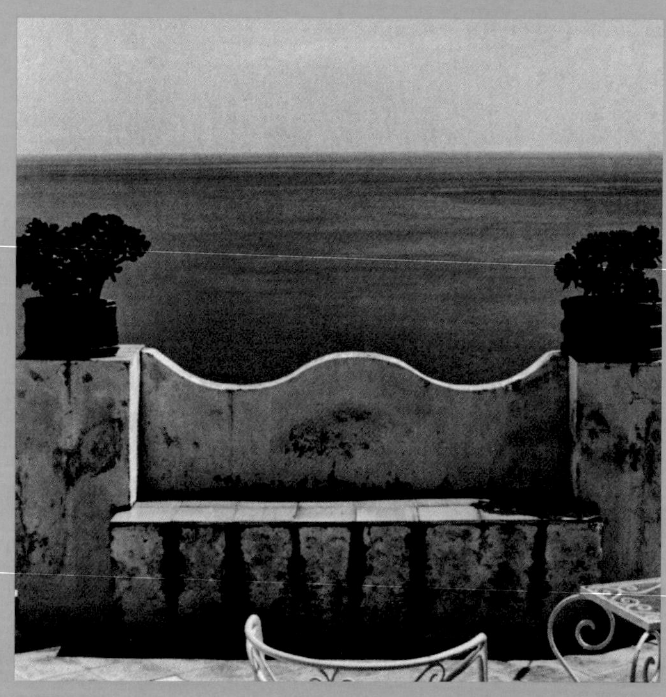

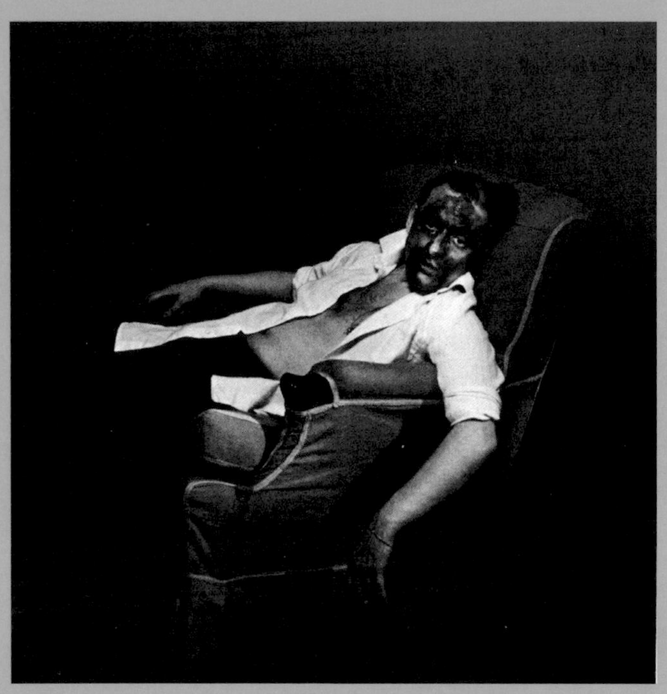

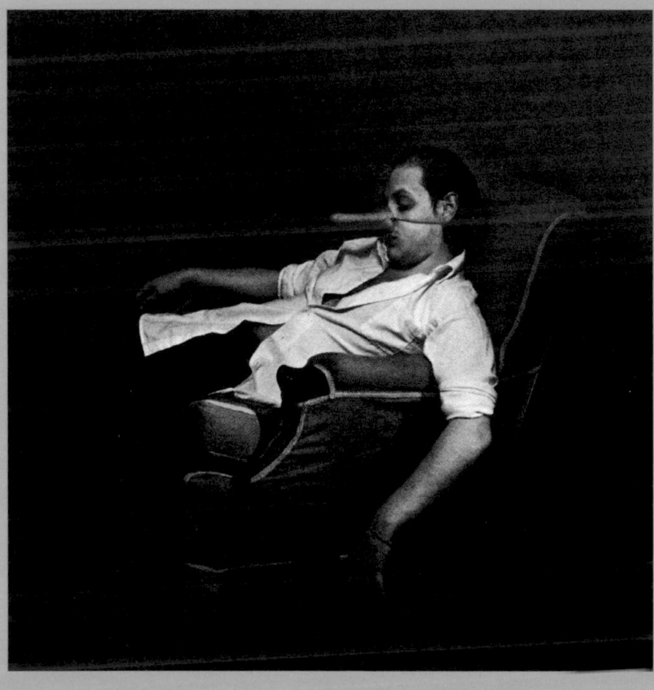

Although I realize that it's no longer possible to create the
same kind of minimalist pieces that my teacher did, I still
draw from this field of personal interest and personal struggle
in my own work, as I try to bring minimalism back to the fore-
front of the art discourse. And this is also true of a student
of mine, Claudia Comte, who makes sculptures that refer back
to minimalism. She has identified what she thinks is lacking
in Sol LeWitt and expands on, renovates, and updates it, taking
the stance that LeWitt is no longer enough. Comte adapts LeWitt's
style to make a plinth for her extremely banal sculpture,

> *Lapin africain 5*, 2014
> Cedar, metal, and car lacquer
> Dimensions variable
> pp. 67-68

Just like Gygi's *Tente-Bar*, you can easily find Comte's wooden
carved sculpture in a flea market. But when installed in this
context, it is very elegant and challenges the formality of
museum display. I find it fascinating the way she is playing
with primitivism. Here is this Swiss girl working in the forest
using a chainsaw, fascinated by virility and the rural sensibility of forest workers. It reminds me of Carl Andre's first
wood pieces. Andre was supposedly working on railroad worksites
and said, "I'm taking back this material." I find that minimalism has always tried to exonerate itself from everything,
to get out of every reference, but in the end, when you look
at the materials they use—the construction materials, the
neon lights—these materials actually say a lot about artists'
macho desires.

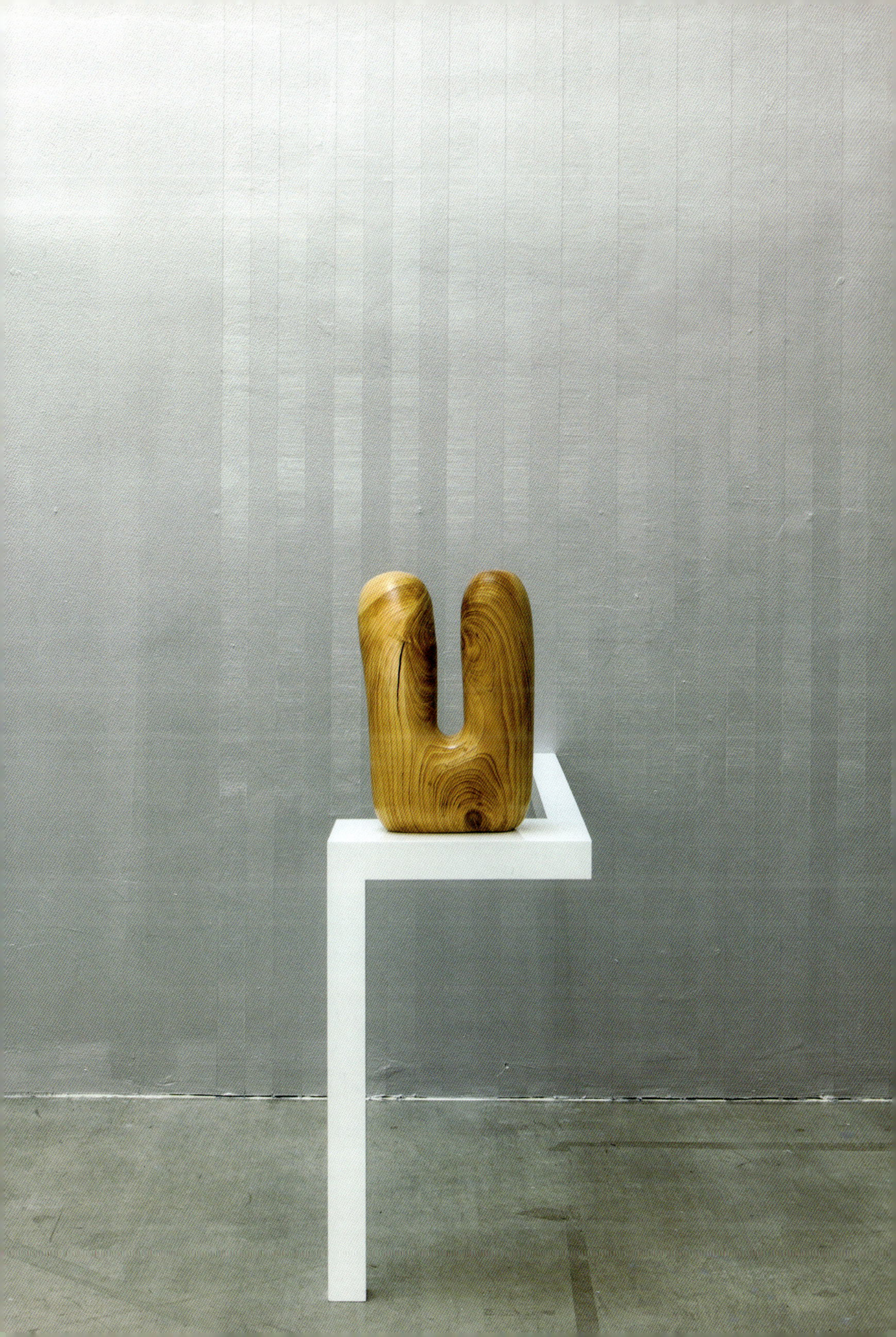

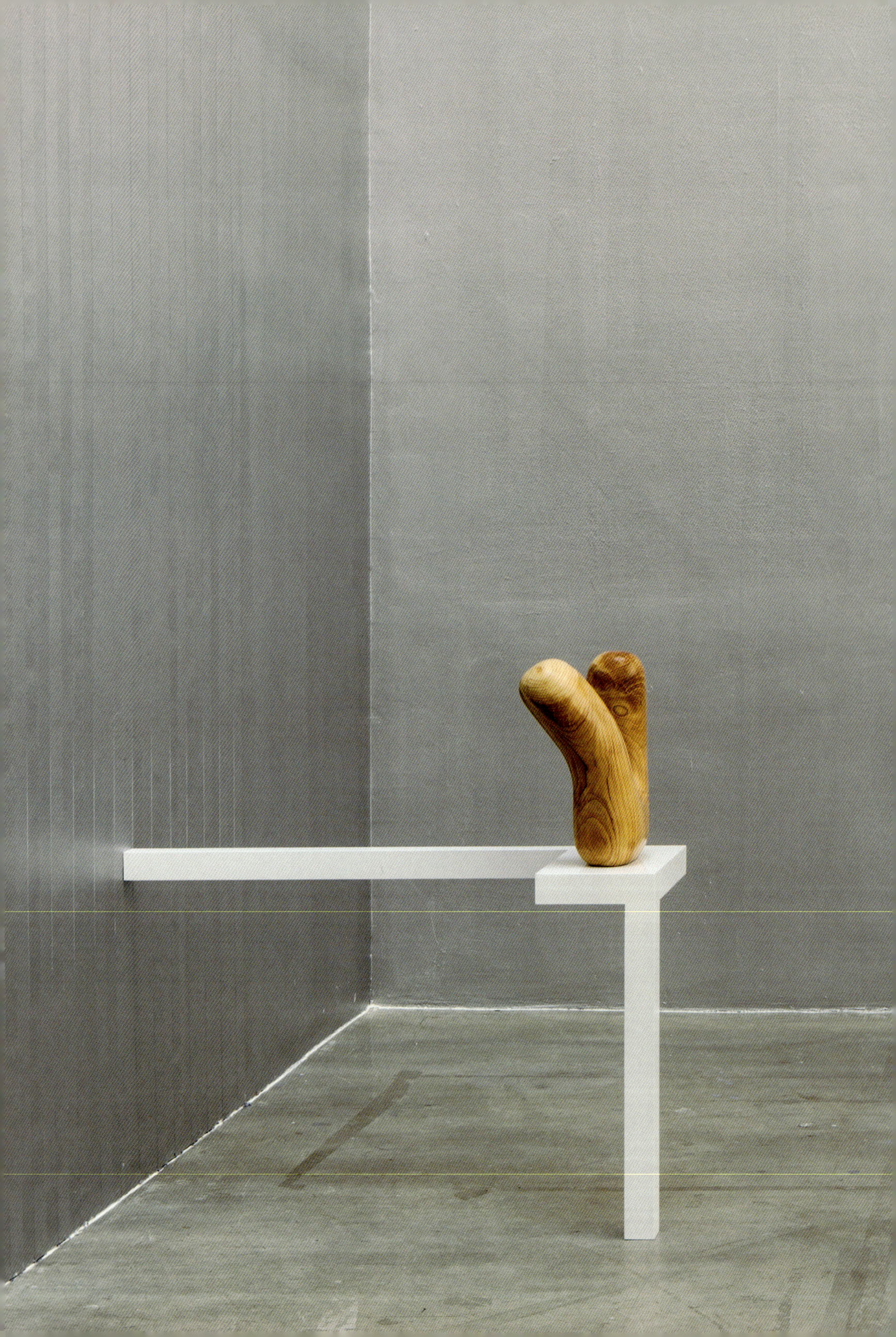

pp. 69, 71: Vittorio Brodmann, *Untitled*, 2013

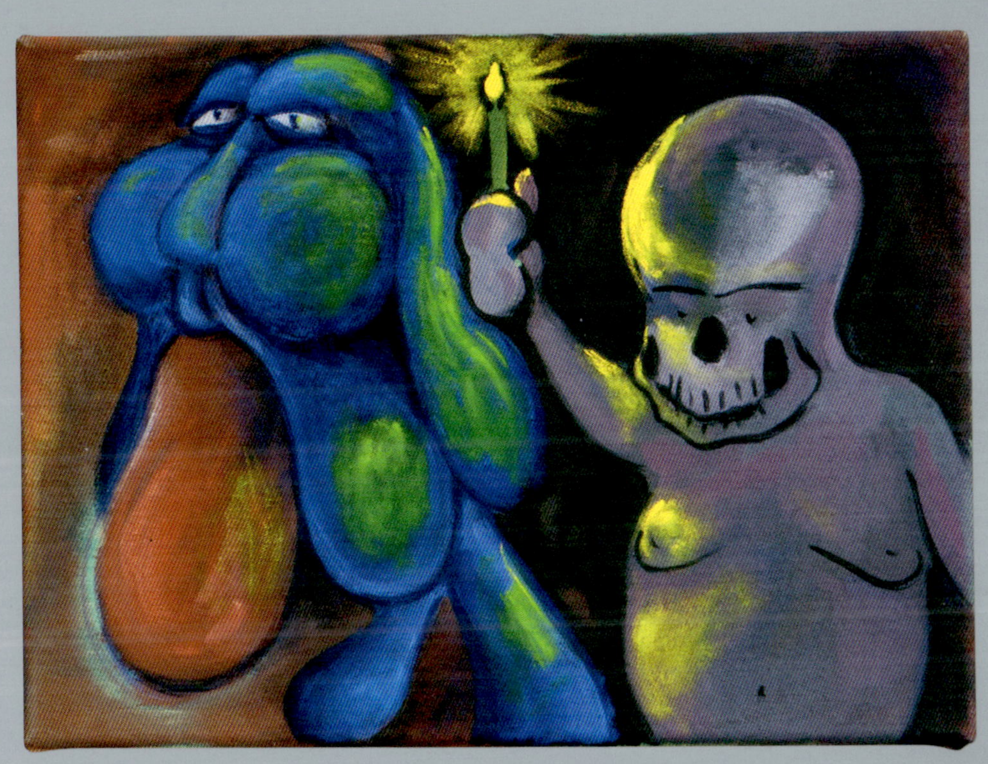

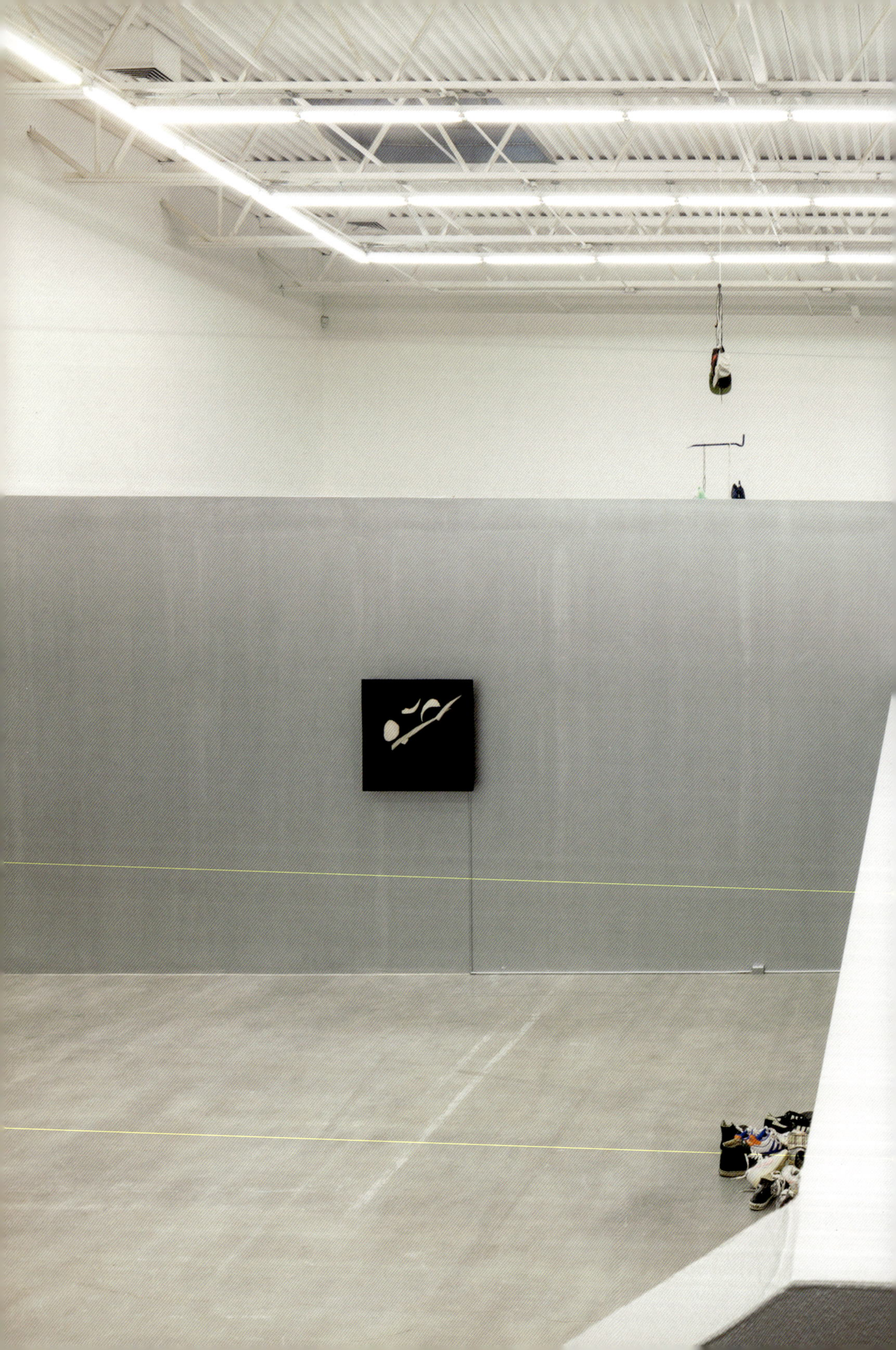

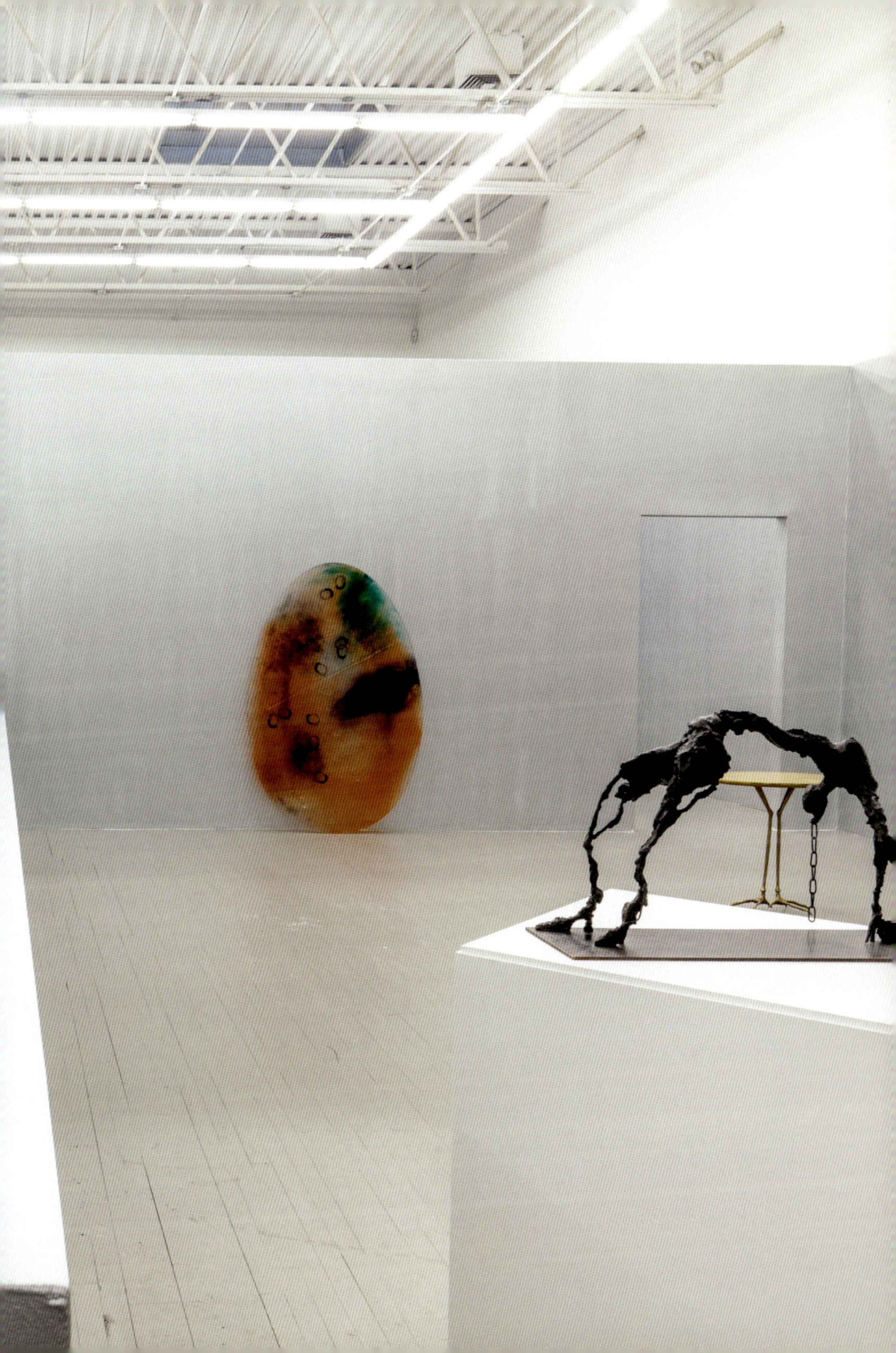

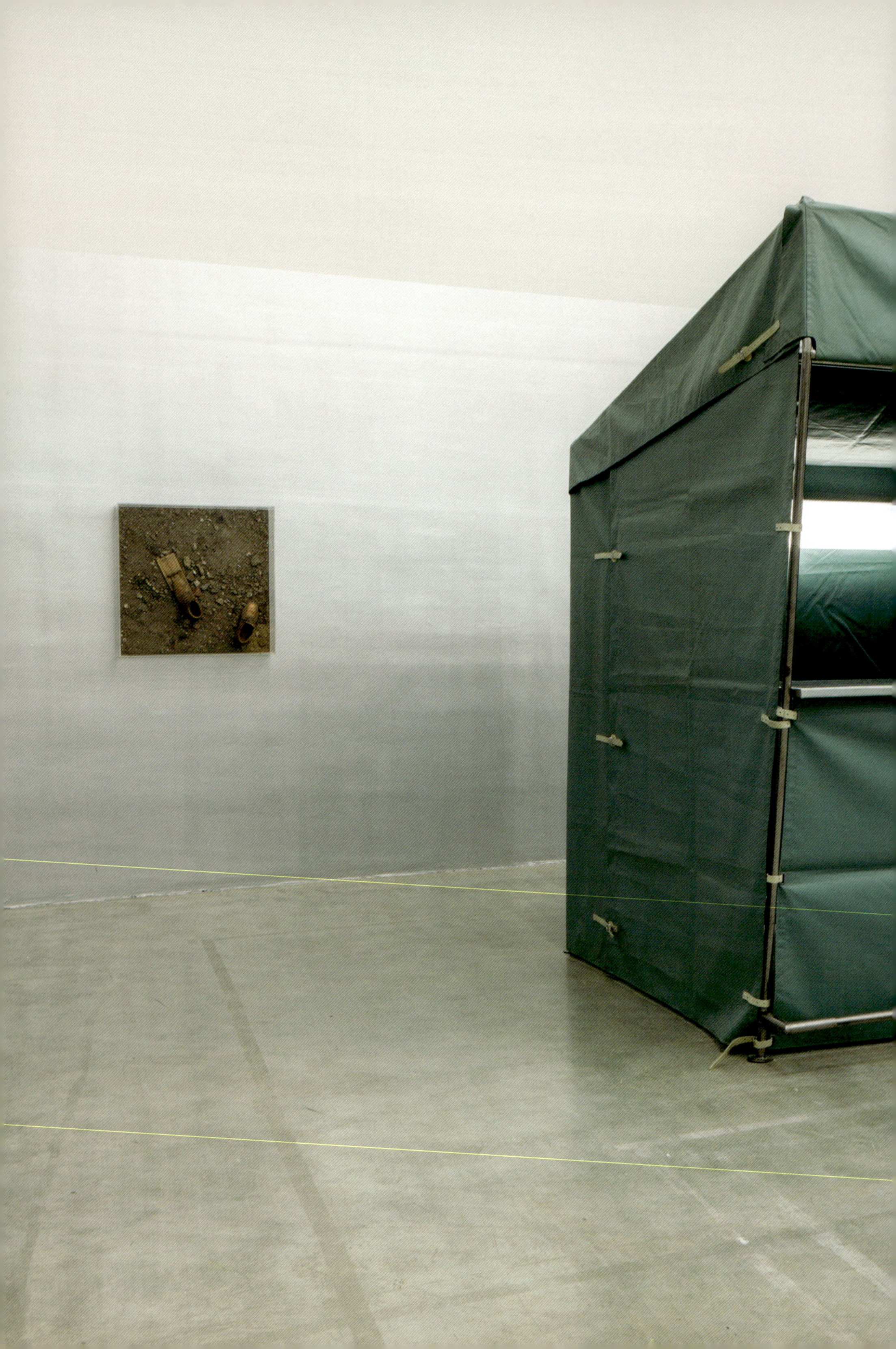

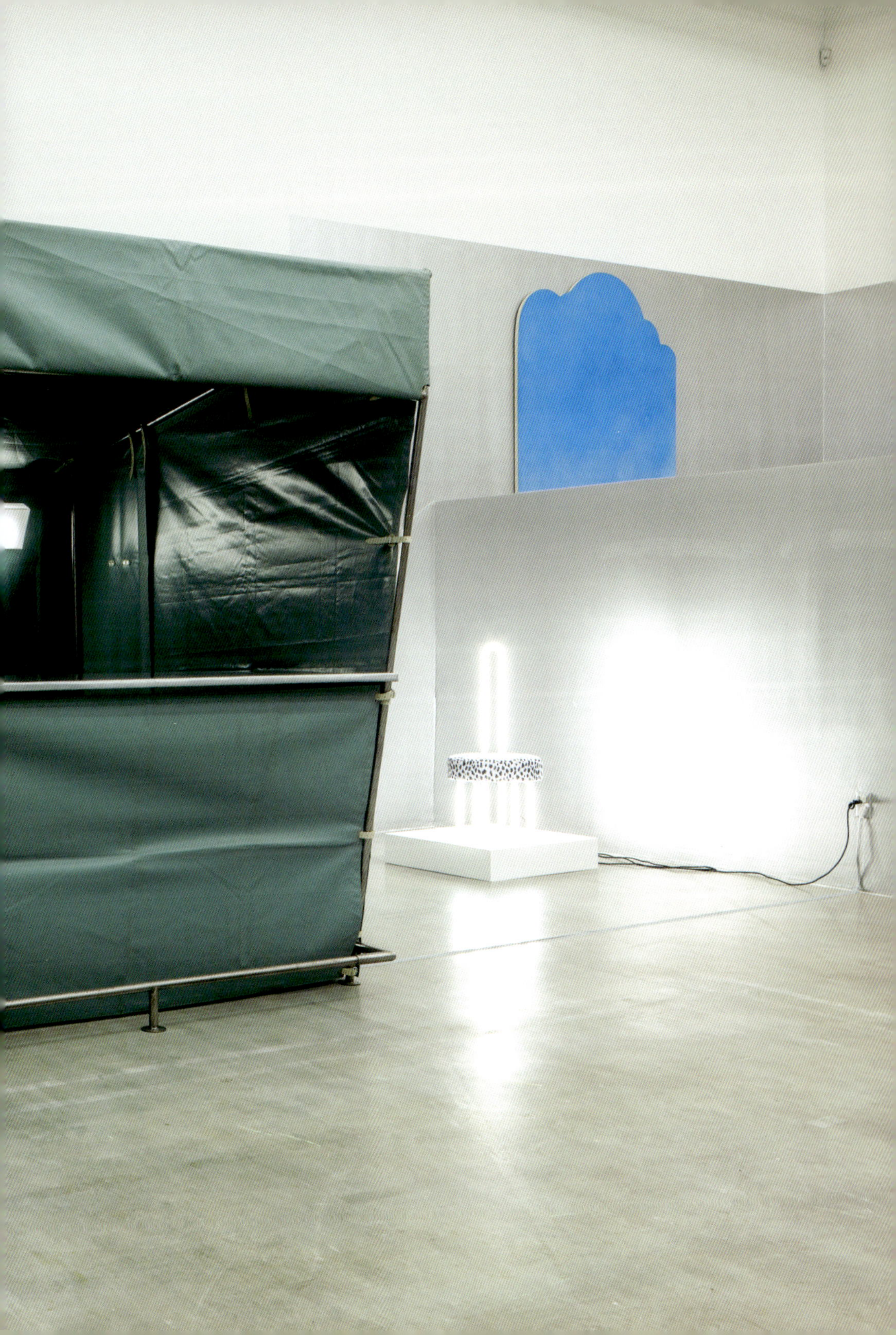

We decided to show Trix and Robert Haussmann's

> *Neon Chair*, 1967
> Fluorescent bulbs and fur
> 23¾ × 23¾ × 39½ inches
> pp. 75, 77

next to Gygi's *Tente-Bar*, which has a neon light as well.
Here the artists play with functionality and the limits of
minimalism, and their work speaks to the uselessness of the
chair. It becomes a representation of the chair, a fascination
with the object. It can't be used, but that's not the point.
They have transformed it. For me, there is almost something
esoteric in the technique they used to make it.

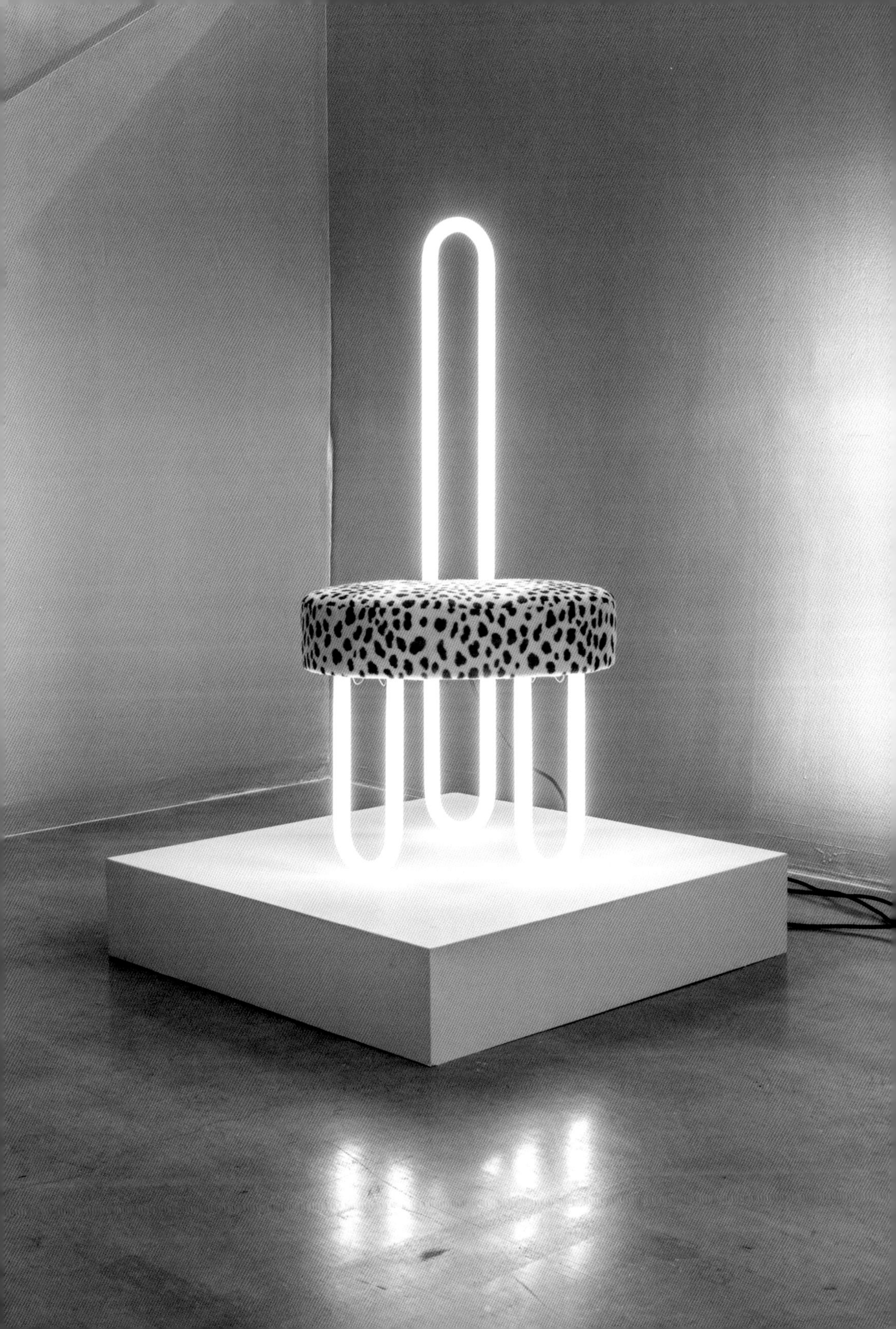

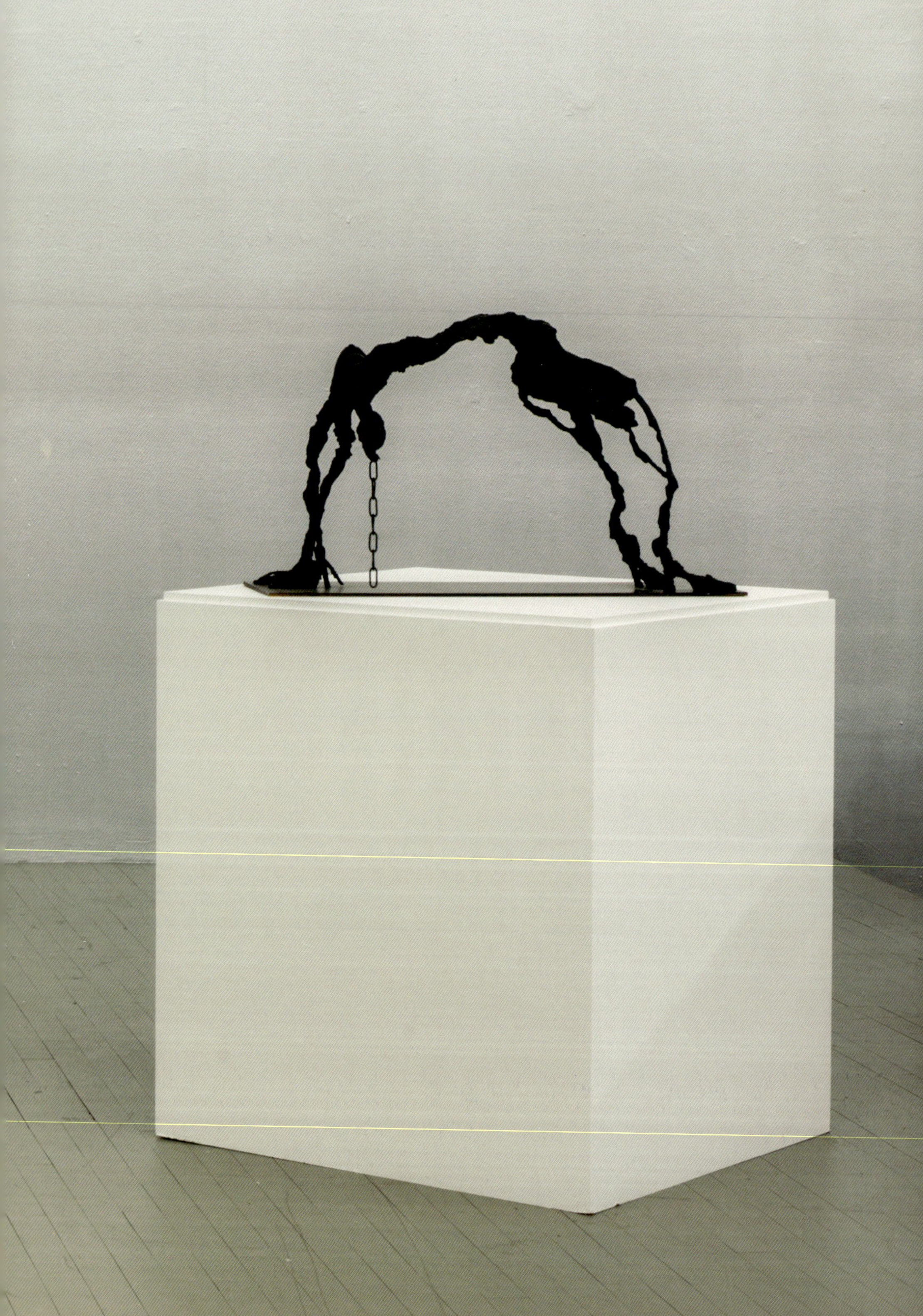

In the last room, there is Luciano Castelli's sculpture,

> *Brücke*, 1994
> Bronze
> 8 × 27¾ × 16½ inches
> pp. 73, 78, 80-81, 83

The meaning of *die brücke* is "the bridge," which means to have hope, to make connections. Die Brücke is also the name of the German expressionist art movement from the beginning of the twentieth century. I don't think that *Brücke* was an innocent choice for the title of this work. This sculpture is pure expressionism, and there is something grossly symbolic about that. Castelli had a certain success in the early 1980s in Berlin. He was part of the Neue Wilde movement, which brought about the reemergence of neo-expressionism in Germany. This sculpture looks like a kind of grotesque man-beast. It reminded me a bit of the S&M beast that appears in Tarantino's *Pulp Fiction*. I also saw references to Alberto Giacometti. Although there's something about it that I find horrible, I also like it. I need it. I like when things don't fit exactly, and I find this piece incongruous in this context. It's an incongruity that I don't understand very well, just as I don't understand why I feel distaste for this work.

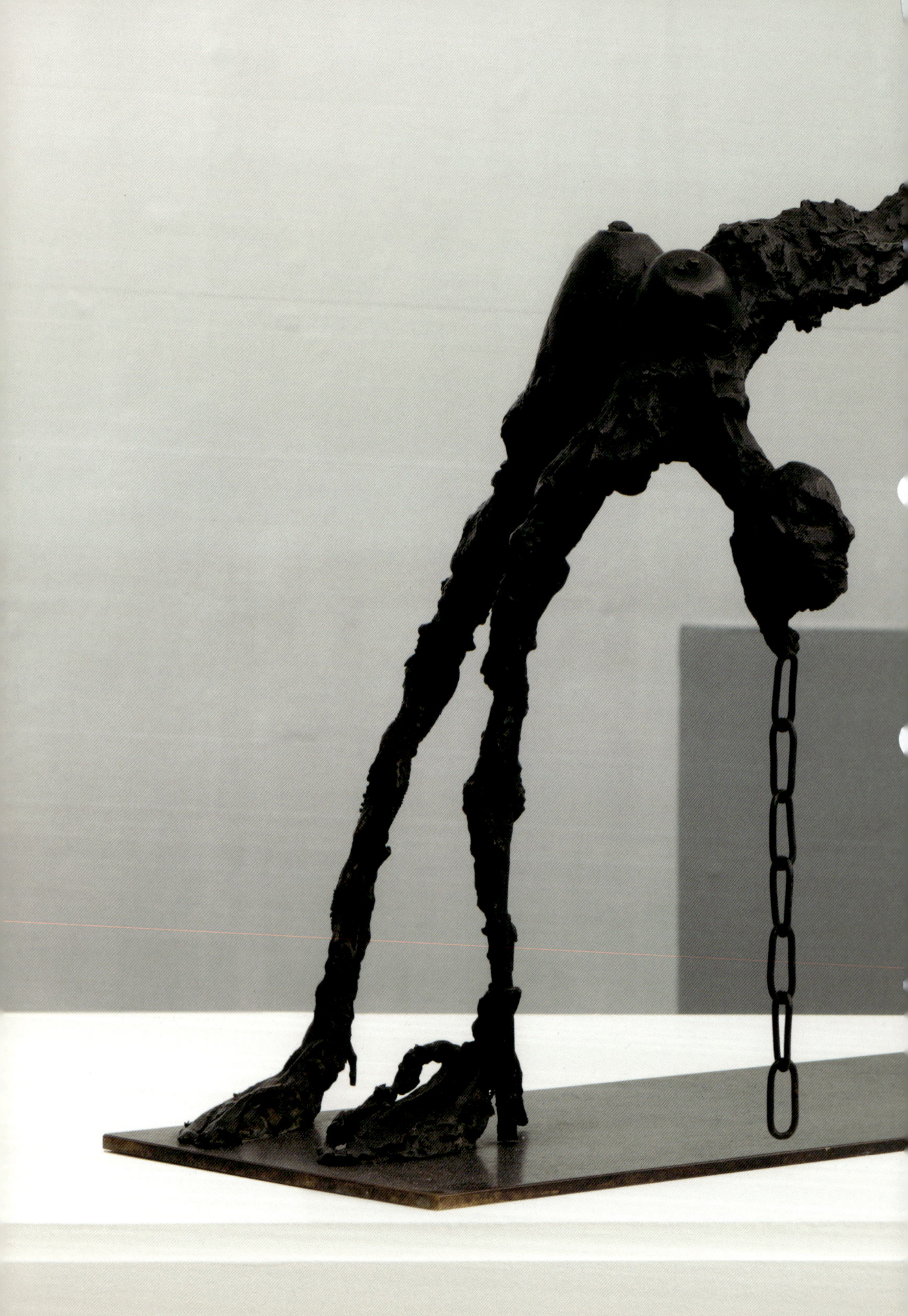

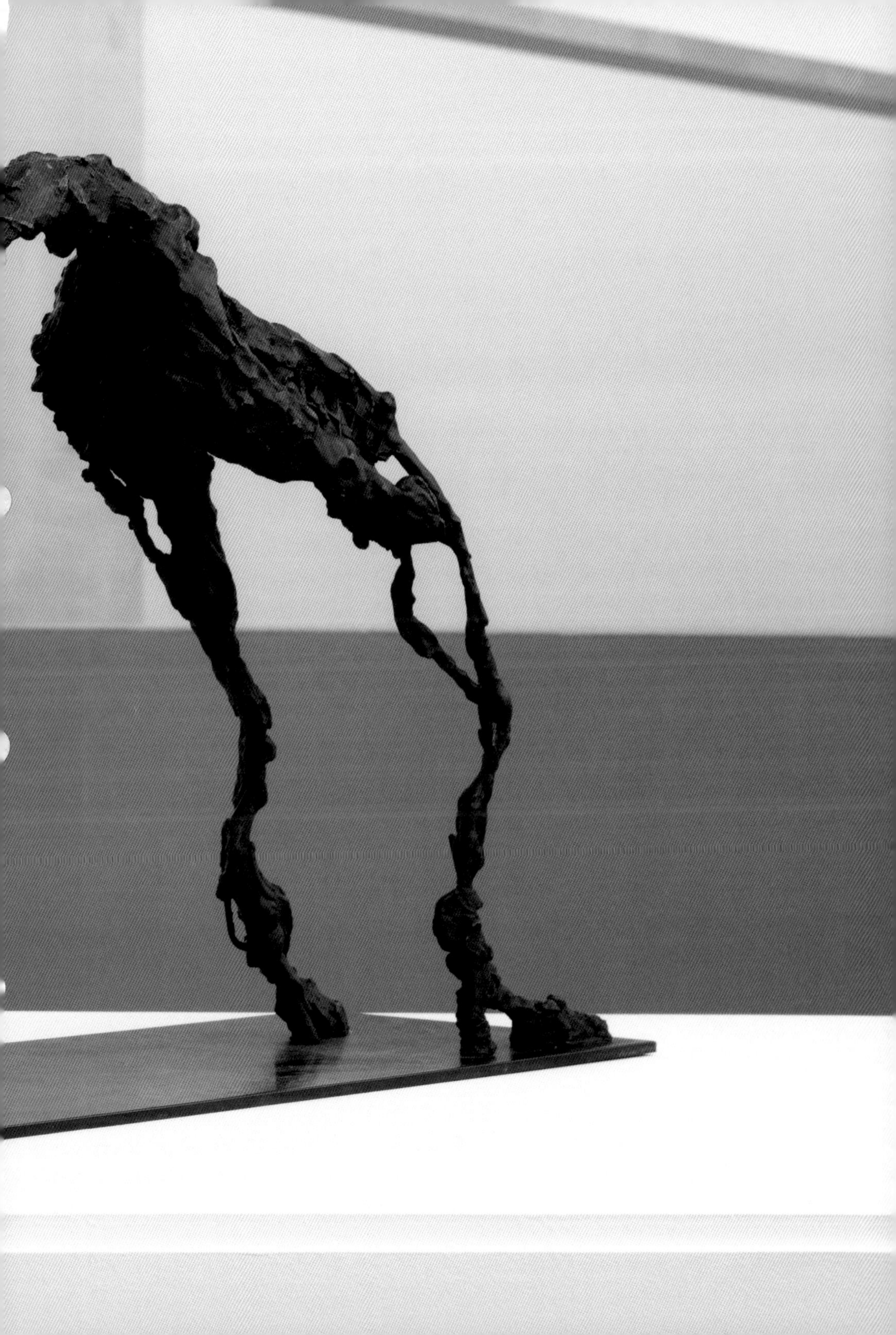

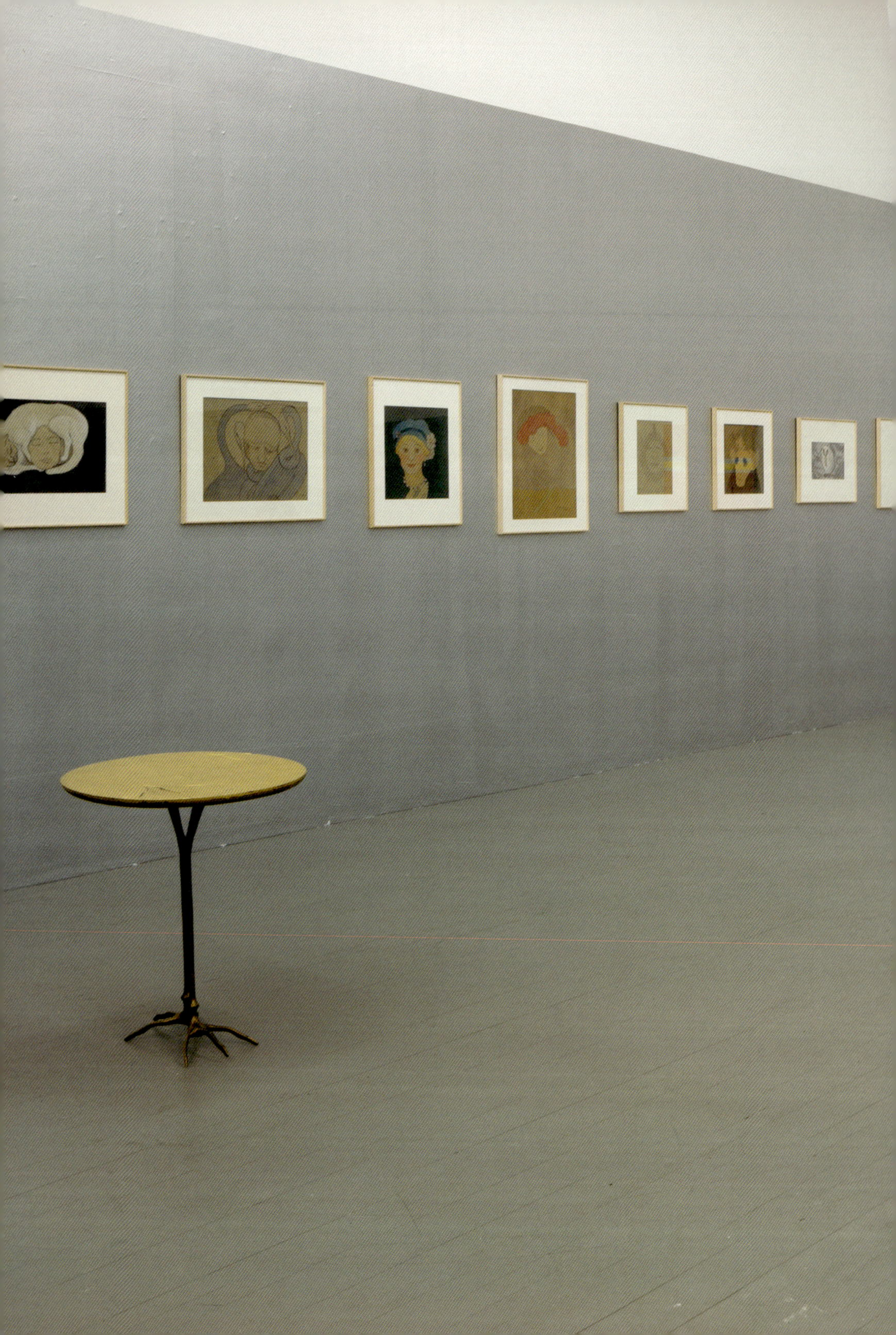

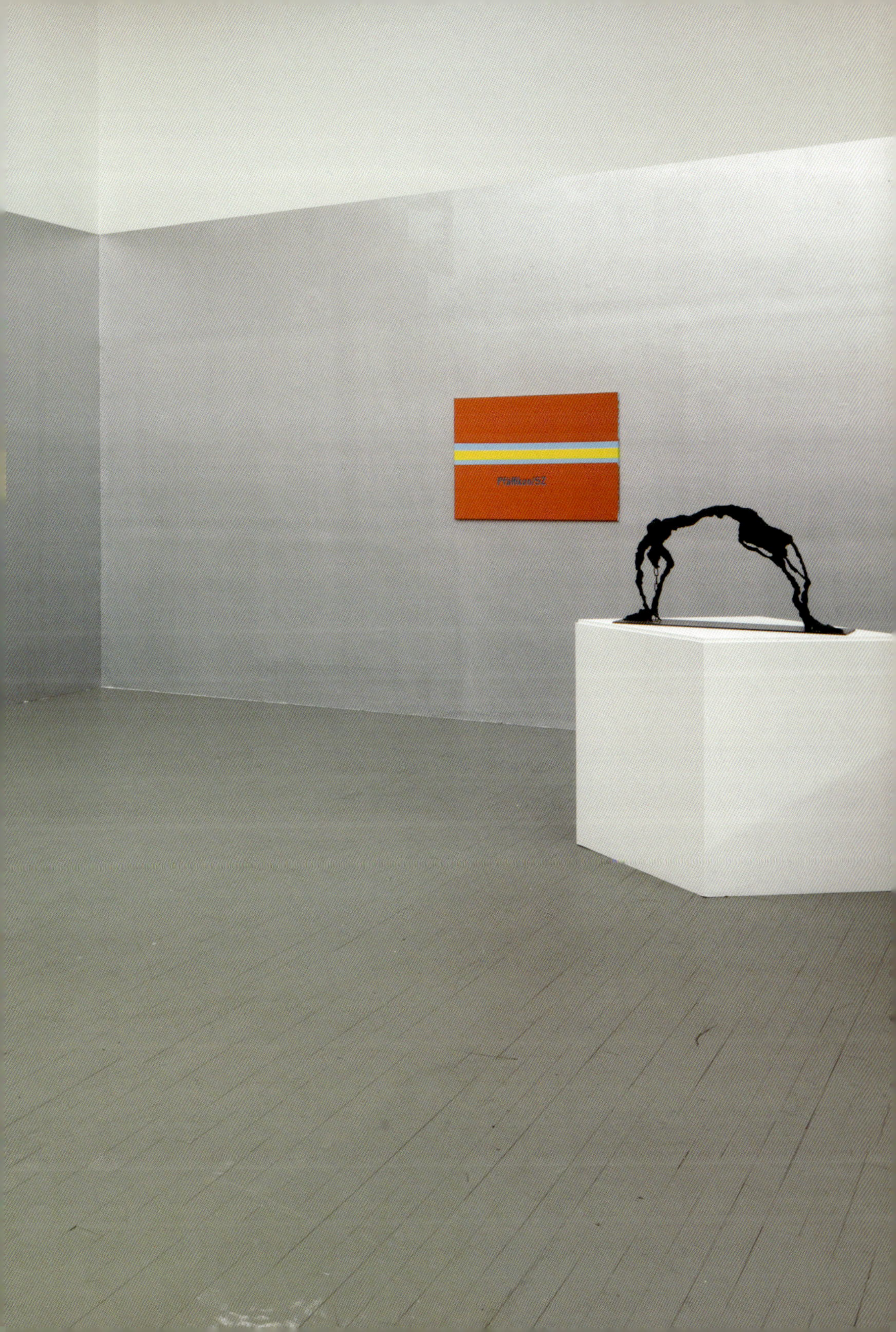

Brücke is in conversation with the painting behind it,
Andreas Hochuli's

> *Pfäffikon/SZ*, 2014
> Acrylic on canvas
> 35½ × 28 inches
> pp. 83, 85

The canvas is rather badly stretched, and it seems to have been
made in a sketchy and brutal way, which seems to nod to the
neo-geometric conceptualism of artists like New York painter
Peter Halley. Pfäffikon is to Zürich what Hoboken is to New
York City—it's a suburb one or two train stops away. It's a
place of boredom, with nothing much going for it. It's hard
to tell what's more banal: this rather aggressive, fluorescent, neo-geo-type painting or the banal town it's named for.
I think it's a question of exaggeration, a reference to minimalism as well as a statement by Hochuli that neo-geo is no
longer enough, and thus this work is a kind of revenge: *I don't
believe in this type of painting anymore, so I'll sabotage it
by linking it to this boring town.* That's what this work says
to me. There's something forsaken, deserted about the painting,
but also humorous and pathetic at the same time. Without the
title, this work could be a painting of a flag, but then all of
a sudden there's the name of this godforsaken place. Here again
is an example of the *spleen* that I described earlier. Affect
corresponds to this type of boring suburban town, juxtaposing
with the idealism that you can do something new. I wanted to
create a situation where there was a painting playing with a
certain ambition, which then pulls the viewer back to the reality of a dull town. And at the same time, as with *Brücke*, the
title contradicts what it is. There is a play between what it
is and what it's meant to be. Both *Brücke* and *Pfäffikon/SZ*
are too much. They're over the top. They've outdone themselves,
but in a way that won't ever be rewarded.

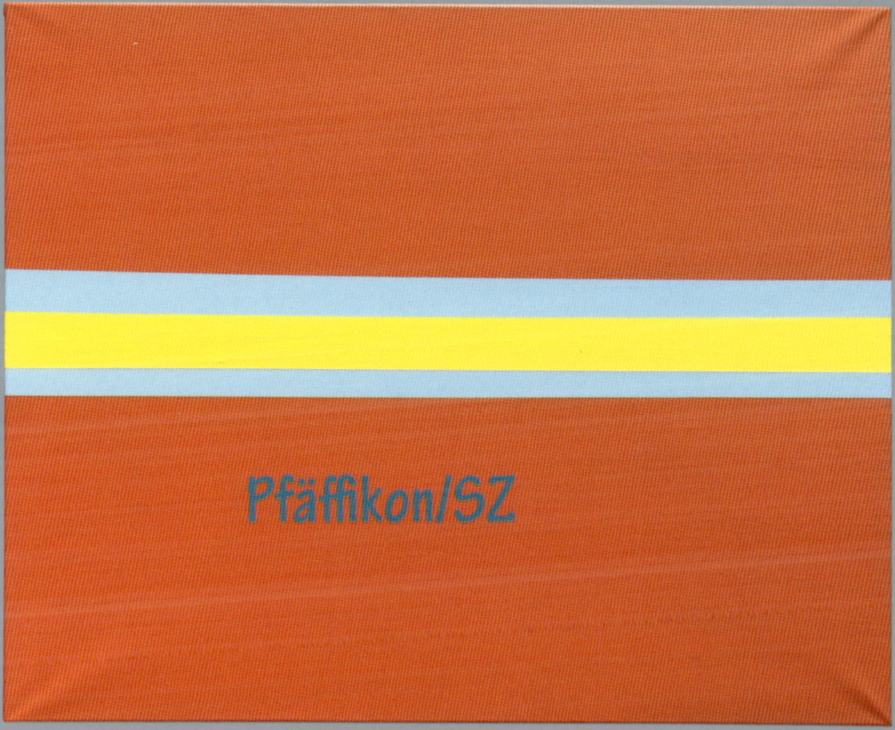

Pfäffikon/SZ

In the end, I prefer to think of *Work Hard* as creating an atmosphere rather than a manifesto. It's more of an intuitive than an intellectual endeavor. I didn't set out to create a neat and tidy construction. As I gathered the pieces, I trusted that they would communicate to each other, that they would mobilize connections across the space. I knew I was bringing together works that were quite heterogeneous. Some works are very recognizable because they have been well-documented. Other works are lesser-known, which grants them the ability to be much more playful. It's impossible to know what was of interest to the people who saw the show. It's very conventional to say this, but I think viewers should always have the freedom to reinterpret the meaning of the exhibition.

As told to Yaniya Lee.

pp. 87, 98: Denis Savary, *Alma (After Kokoschka)*, 2007

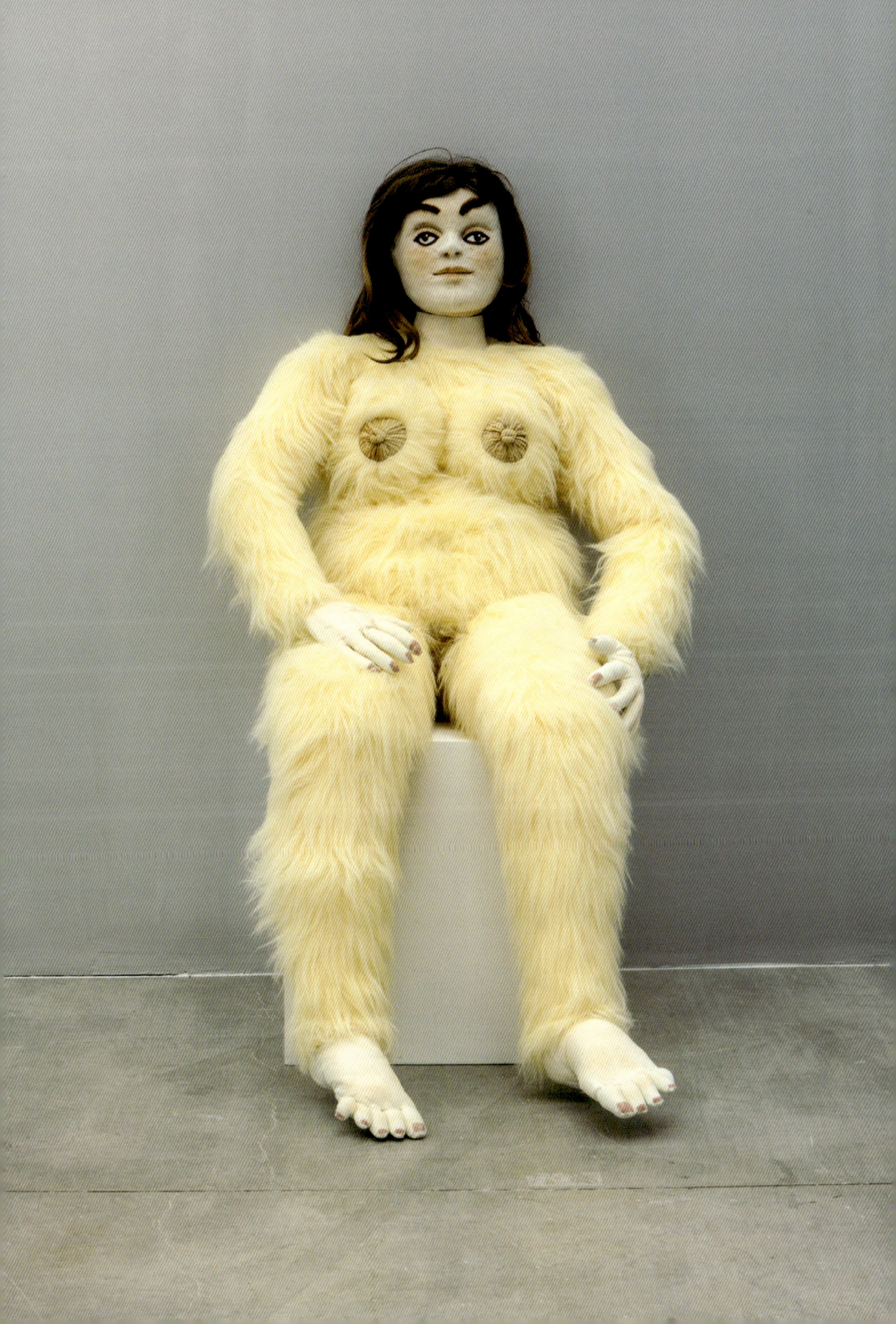

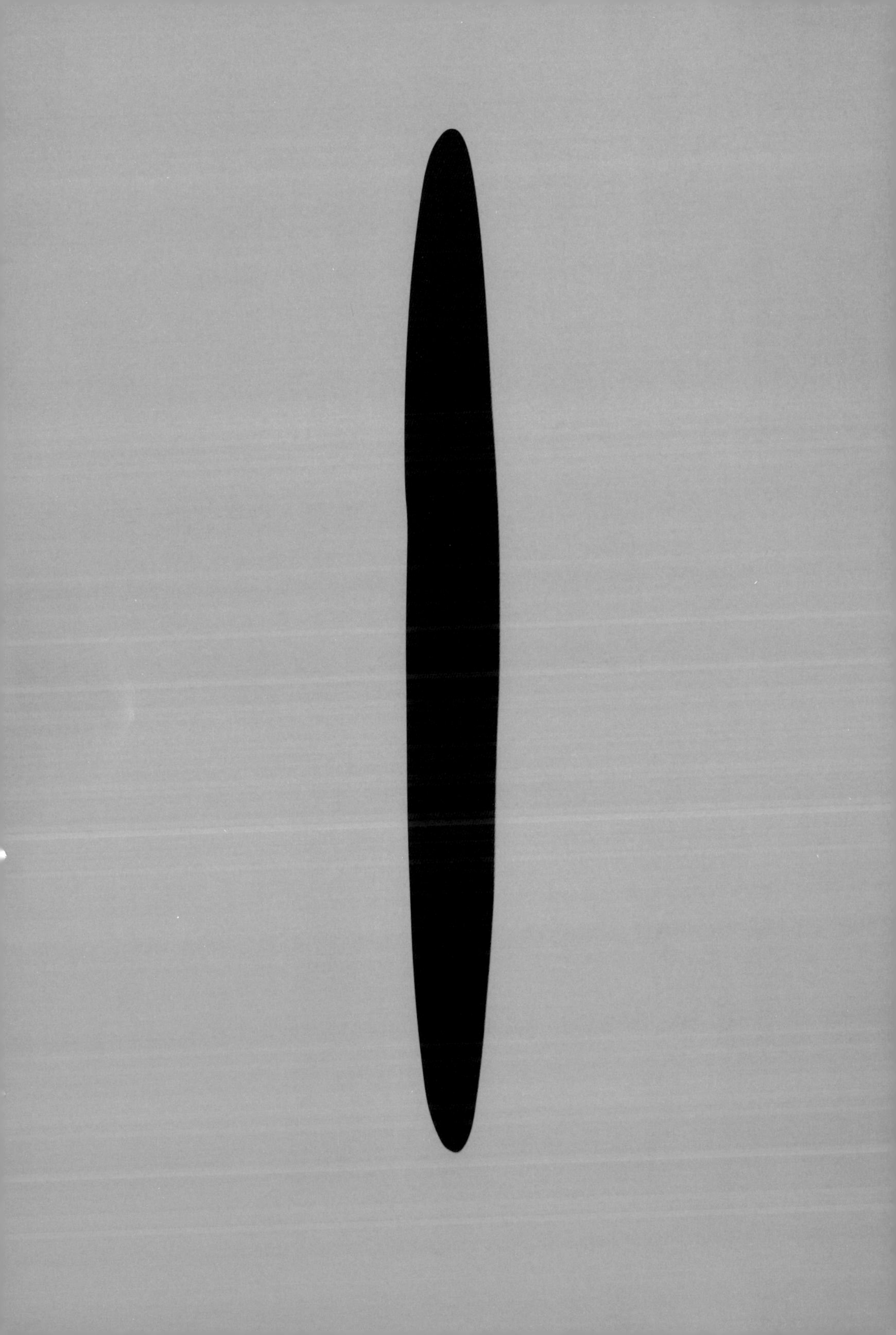

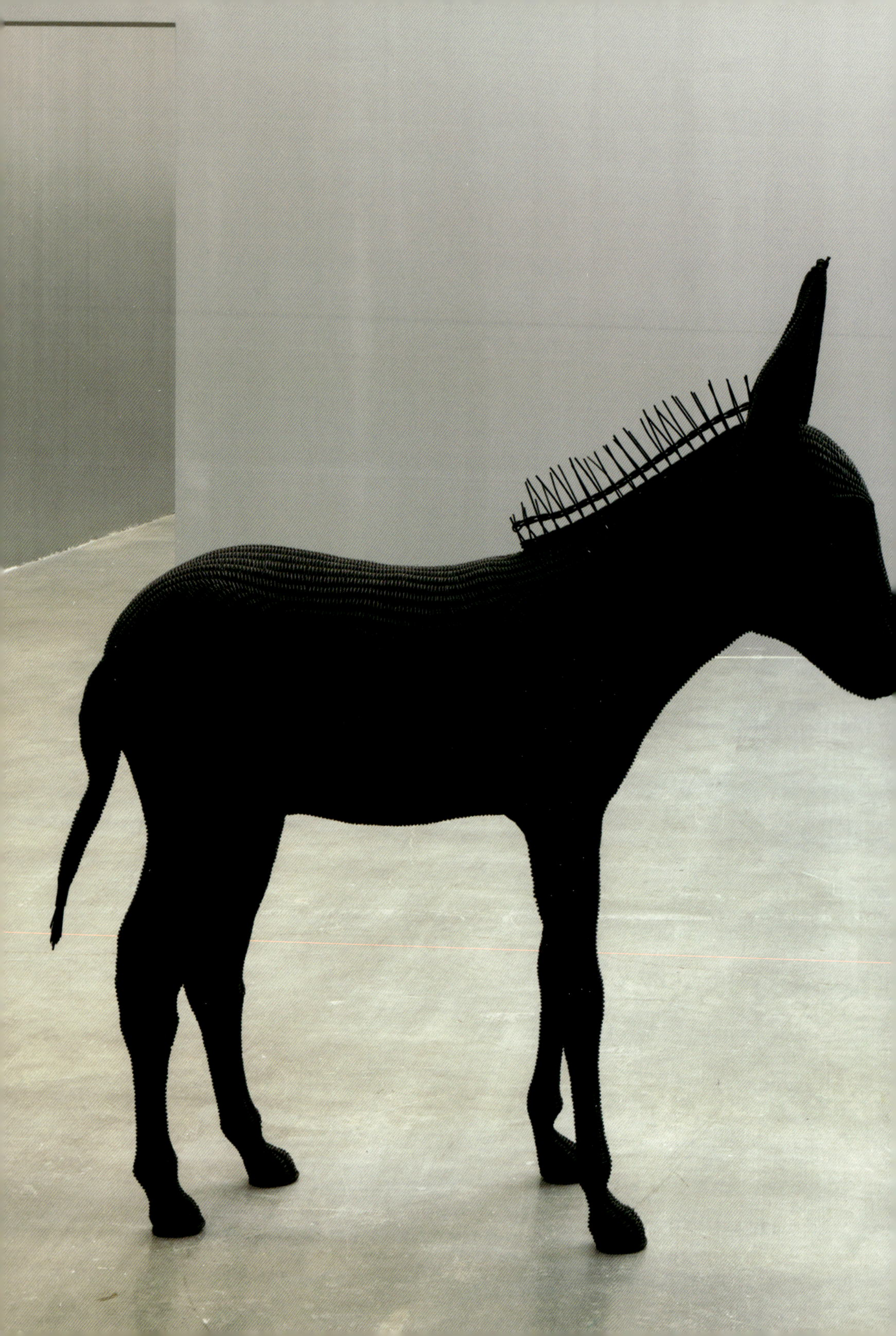

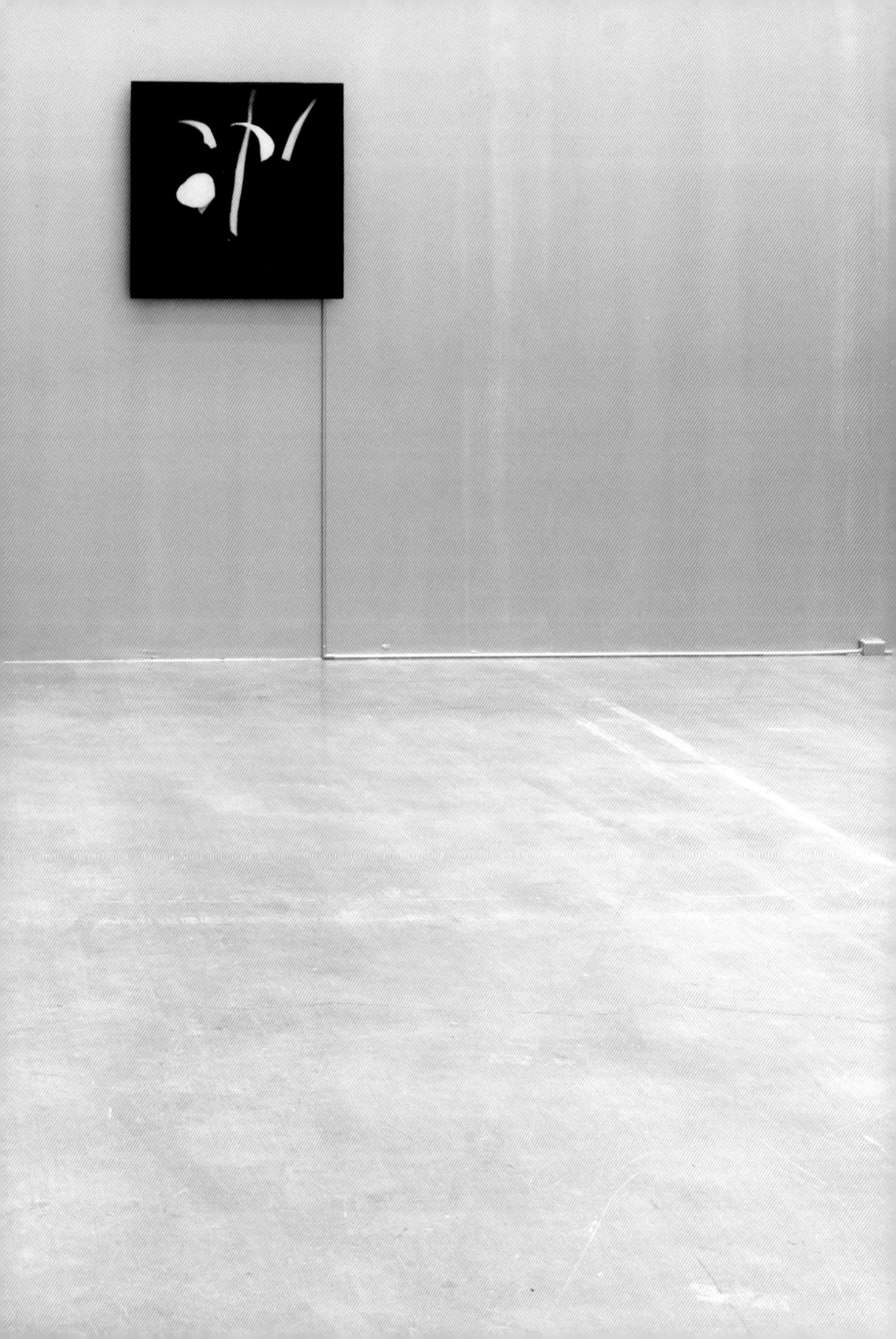

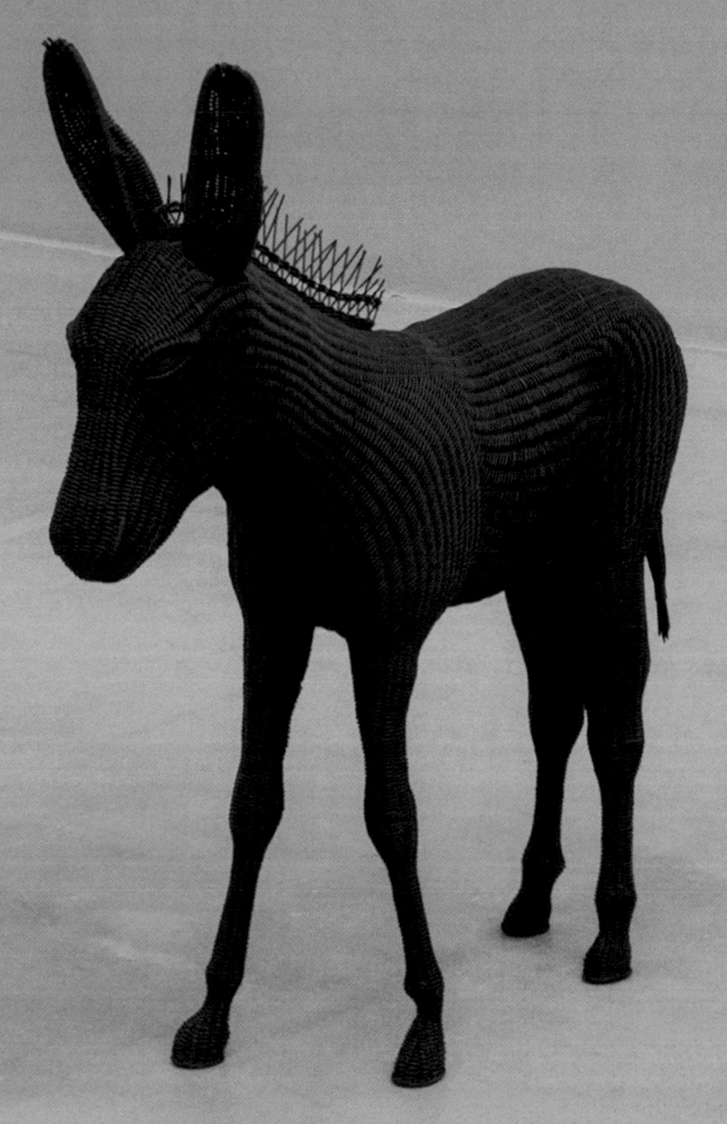

Untitled
Mai-Thu Perret

ALPINE CRETINISM

"I've always hated Vorarlberg, as I have Switzerland, where
cretinism reigns supreme, as my father always said, on this
point I didn't disagree with him. I knew Chur from my frequent
visits there with my parents, that is, when we were traveling
to St. Moritz and would spend the night in Chur, always in
the same hotel, which stank of peppermint tea and where the
hotel management knew my father and gave him a twenty percent
discount because he had *remained faithful to the hotel for
over forty years*. It was a so-called good hotel, in the center
of town, I no longer remember the name, perhaps it was the
Sunshine Inn, if I'm not mistaken, although it was located
in the murkiest spot in town. The taverns in Chur served the
worst wine and the most tasteless sausages. My father always
had dinner with us in the hotel, ordered a so-called appetizer
and called Chur *a pleasant stopover point*, which I never
understood, for I had always found Chur particularly distaste-
ful. Even more than the Salzburgers, the Churians struck me as
despicable in their Alpine cretinism. I always felt as if I were
being punished when I had to go to St. Moritz with my parents,
sometimes only with my father, had to stop over in Chur, had to
stay in that dreary hotel with windows looking out on a narrow,
dank street. In Chur I had never been able to sleep, I thought,
I had always lain awake in complete despair. Chur is actually
the gloomiest place I've ever seen, not even Salzburg is as
gloomy and, in the final analysis, as sickening as Chur. And the
Churians are just the same. A person can be ruined for life in
Chur, even if he spends only one night there."
—Thomas Bernhard[1]

PSYCHOGEOGRAPHY

It's a kind of critical cliché to examine an artist-curated
exhibition in terms of self-portraiture. By assembling artworks
that she likes or feels an affinity for, the artist is supposedly revealing something about herself and what makes her tick.
In *Work Hard*, however, Valentin Carron sidesteps the construction
of a narrative of artistic and sensitive individuality and

instead sketches a territory—the outline of a personally and politically inflected geography. This terrain, roughly speaking, is called Switzerland. Not the postcard Switzerland of mountain vistas and sublime landscapes, but rather that of the spaces in-between: the long valleys and suburban plains where midsize towns flow into one another, often dank and gloomy like the town of Chur in Graubünden, which Thomas Bernhard took such obvious pleasure in eviscerating.

LOCAL HISTORIES

Work Hard sketches a singular genealogy of influence, juxtaposing the familiar avant-garde—such as Méret Oppenheim or Daniel Spoerri—with more regional figures like Edmond Bille and Marguerite Burnat-Provins. Bille was a prolific painter and engraver who fell in love with the canton of Valais at the turn of the twentieth century. He designed and built for himself a castle in the romantic style on the edge of Sierre. He personified the idea of the artist as benevolent patriarch and patriot, able to play medieval lord in his castle while defending socialist ideas and mingling with pacifist intellectuals. His folio *Une danse macabre*, published in 1919, is a passionate testimony against the horrors of the Great War. A painter and writer who was also struck by the beauty of Valais, Burnat-Provins is a more troubled figure, no doubt in part because her gender did not allow her the same freedom as Bille. To this day, the canton of Valais remains the most fiercely Catholic one in the country. A divorcée, Burnat-Provins was the object of a public scandal and was forced to leave the town of Savièse when her in-laws refused to recognize her second wedding in 1906. The victim of frequent hallucinations, she began, at the outbreak of the First World War, a series of more than three thousand drawings she called "Ma Ville" (1914–52). Created under the influence of the spirits who dictated their contents, the drawings are populated by nightmarish half-animal, half-human creatures.

BORDER CONTROLS

In Mathis Gasser's painting *Superstructures for Europe* (2012), a runny, washy outline of the continent is overlaid with a diagonal double-cross. The cross is nonspecific, and it is this generic quality—as reminiscent of a Lorraine cross as a motif on the cover of a Scandinavian death-metal album—that gives it its power. The painting's effect is that of a not-so-repressed fragment of the collective European unconscious, complete with memories of past conflicts, conflicts that have the potential to be reawakened at any moment. Throughout the exhibition there

are repeated nods to a kind of dull, standardized, and slightly
fascistic common order, and the definition of masculinity
that this entails. Fabrice Gygi's *Tente-Bar* (1997) is a tarpaulin and steel shelter reminiscent of the kind of structures
laid out for public festivities, such as commercial parties
like Zürich's Street Parade, or celebrations for the end of the
grape harvest in more rural areas. It is also reminiscent of
structures built in army encampments or in refugee camps, and
the similarities between spaces of "play" and those of war are
no accident. The ideology of the militia, where every male cit-
izen is a dormant soldier, although no longer functional in the
organization of the army, still plays a powerful role in the
national imagination of collectivity and control. This supposed
Swiss exceptionalism is invoked time and again by nationalist
and populist politicians during campaigns against the European
Union or immigration.

WHAT IS SCULPTURE FOR I

"Yesterday I sent a life-size drawing of my beloved and I ask
you to copy this most carefully and to transform it into reality. Pay special attention to the dimensions of the head and
neck, to the ribcage, the rump, and the limbs. And take to
heart the contours of body, e.g., the line of the neck to the
back, the curve of the belly. Please permit my sense of touch
to take pleasure in those places where layers of fat or muscle
suddenly give way to a sinewy covering of skin. For the first
layer (inside) please use fine, curly horsehair; you must
buy an old sofa or something similar; have the horsehair dis-
infected. Then, over that, a layer of pouches stuffed with
down, cottonwool for the seat and breasts. The point of all
this for me is an experience which I must be able to embrace!"
—Oskar Kokoschka, letter to Hermine Moos, August 20, 1918 [2]

Denis Savary's *Alma* (2007) is a re-creation, from descriptions
and photographs, of the doll that the Austrian expressionist
painter Oskar Kokoschka had fashioned as an effigy of his
former lover and model, Alma Mahler. Shortly after receiving
the doll from her maker, Kokoschka started taking her to
the theater and painting portraits of her, but after a year
he ultimately grew tired of the surrogate and finally destroyed
it during a drunken party, declaring his erotic obsession over.

WORK HARD

The gold tinsel wrapper looks like something you'd find around
cheese or sweets. It's attached to a pink clothespin holding
a delicate tail of crumpled train tickets and store receipts.

A small plastic skull has been stuck inside the clothespin like a stud, and the whole thing balances, fan-like, on top of a long, whitewashed stick. On the same plinth, there are three other assemblages of found, everyday objects, each placed on pedestals made from cans of paint thinner. The cans are roughly painted white, and topped, respectively, with mussel shells; three used, black plastic lighters with photographic motifs of euro coins and diamonds; and a used crack pipe mounted atop a grape stem, frosty with epoxy. These four sculptures by David Hominal (*Animal with Baggage*, 2010) are deliberate, miniature altars to the cracked and the discarded, melancholy haiku to the artist as idler and unproductive member of society.

WHAT IS SCULPTURE FOR II

Emerentia 1713 (1979) is a novella by S. Corinna Bille set in eighteenth-century Valais—in Fully, a village in the Rhône Valley that also happens to be Valentin Carron's hometown. It's the story of a little girl abandoned by her father and stepmother to an abusive priest, who believes she is possessed by the devil. Emerentia is a beautiful, rebellious child, and her instinctive connection to the natural world arouses the puritanical fury of her guardians, who sadistically torture her to death under the pretense of saving her soul. In many ways Emerentia resembles Mouchette, the heroine of the eponymous 1967 Robert Bresson film about a solitary young girl who is abused and ostracized by everyone in her small French village and ends up drowning herself. My sculpture *Black Balthazar* (2013) is a baby donkey made out of wicker. It was named after another Bresson film, *Au Hasard Balthazar* (1966), whose hero is a donkey subjected to all manner of brutality and abuse at the hands of men. Of course, in Christian mythology the donkey is symbolically associated with Christ and the Virgin Mary, both of whom it carries. He is the beast of burden, the poor man's horse, a mute figure of love, labor, and patience.

Notes

1. Thomas Bernhard, *The Loser*, trans. Jack Dawson (New York: Vintage International, 2006), 59-60.

2. Oskar Kokoschka, as quoted in Sadie Stein, "My Fair Lady," *The Paris Review*, February 17, 2015, http://www.theparisreview.org/blog/2015/02/17/my-fair-lady/.

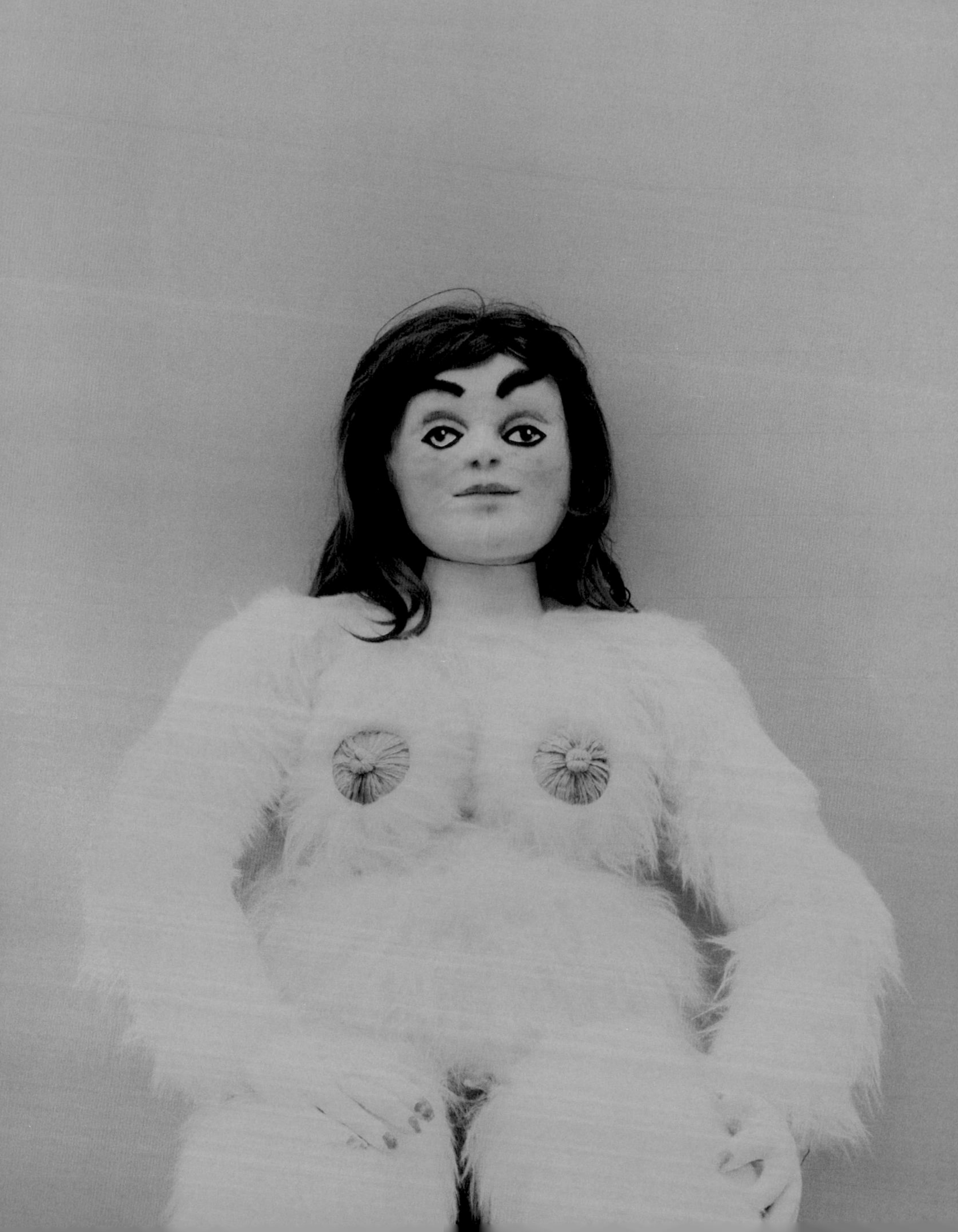

The Immortal Bodies
Boris Groys

In our present time, one feels somewhat embarrassed when speaking or writing of immortality, in particular the immortality of an individual. You feel you have to explain how on earth you came up with such an odd—even kitsch—topic. Today, the individual's immortality seems a more appropriate theme for a Hollywood B movie than for a seriously wrought philosophical essay. This has not always been the case. In the past, it was not considered uncomfortable to talk about immortality because people believed that the soul would outlive the body. Therefore, it was considered absolutely appropriate and reasonable to give thought, while still on earth, as to where your soul would end up when you died. But above all, our ancestors would pose the question of which part of the soul was potentially immortal—and which part was mortal.

Philosophy, as it was initiated by Plato, has been for a long period of history nothing other than an attempt to anticipate the further life of the soul after death. In other words, it has been expected to carry out a metanoia; that is, a transition from an innerworldly to an otherworldly perspective, from the perspective of the mortal body to that of the eternal soul. Metanoia is a necessary starting point from which to become metaphysical, to attain a metaposition in relation to the world and thus to regard and think of the world as a whole. If the metanoia—that is, the anticipation of one's own immortality—becomes impossible, the individual loses the ability to change perspectives. In this case, the only starting point for an individual's thinking and praxis is the perspective with which every individual is issued through his inner nature and the terrestrial positioning of his body. If one is merely mortal, to escape one's position in the world is impossible.

Today, though, as modern, post-Enlightenment individuals, we hold that God is dead and that the soul cannot outlive the body. Or, to be more precise, we do not believe that such a thing as a soul can actually be differentiated from the body—separated, made independent. Correspondingly, we also do not believe that a change of perspective, a metanoia—that is, achievement of a metaposition in relation to the world—is possible. Of anyone who speaks today, it is first asked where he is from and from which perspective he speaks. Race, class, and gender serve as coordinates whereby the positioning of every voice is located. The concept of cultural identity, which stands at the center of today's "cultural studies," also serves this same initial positioning. Even though the relevant parameters and identities are interpreted as social constructs rather than "natural" determinants, this hardly invalidates their effect. It may perhaps be possible to deconstruct social constructions, but they cannot be abolished or deliberately replaced.

Still, it seems to me that the finitude of the soul does not yet mean that metanoia is impossible. Even in modernity there has been no perfect synchronization of body and soul: both remain heterochronic and thus separable, despite the loss of faith in the soul's immortality. Although we no longer speak of a disembodied soul, still we can and must speak of a soul-less body, or a corpse. The soul may have no further life after the death of the body; however, the body certainly lives on after the soul passes away. Here, we can definitely speak of a life after death, because a corpse is active throughout: after death, it remains active in that it elapses, decays, and decomposes. This process of decay is potentially infinite—one cannot definitively say when the process ends because the body's material substances remain identifiable for a long enough time. Even if the vestiges of the corpse can no longer be identified, it doesn't mean the body has disappeared, but simply that its elements—molecules, atoms, et cetera—have dispersed throughout the world to such an extent that the body has practically become one with the entire world. If you wish, it has become a body without organs.

This unification with the cosmos, materially as well as spiritually, offers a perspective that makes possible another kind of metanoia. Instead of the immortality of the soul, we achieve a different kind of immortality: that of the body's material substances—of the body as a corpse. This corporeal immortality can be anticipated during one's own life as much as the eternal life of the soul was anticipated in the past. Perhaps here we can speak of a heteronoia, an anticipation of the body's rather than the soul's destiny in the afterlife. Moreover, we could even argue that the concept of corporeal immortality is older than the belief in the immortality of the soul: Egyptian rituals of mummification tell us nothing else.

I am speaking here of heteronoia after Michel Foucault's concept of heterotopia. Once the soul has departed, the body as corpse is transported to the cemetery, a space other than the one it occupied during its life. Foucault rightfully considers the cemetery, along with the museum, the library, and the boat—we could also add the garbage heap here—as "other" places, as heterotopiae.[1] The body transcends the place where it resided during its lifetime in that it has been brought to the cemetery. As a result, a pretty drastic change of perspective takes place: looking out from a cemetery, a museum, or a library, the world appears from a different—a heterotopic—perspective. In this way, it is possible for the individual to experience heteronoia by thinking of his body, during his lifetime, as a corpse. Then we wouldn't ask where he is coming from, but where he will be brought after his death—and thus this heterotopic end point becomes the origin of his worldview.

Philosophy has been preoccupied for a long time with the meta-physics of the corpse—whether explicitly or implicitly. There is no other way of understanding the entire Decadent movement of the nineteenth century. In *The Origin of German Tragic Drama* (1928), Walter Benjamin describes allegory as a figure that represents the body's decay. Thus, allegory, for Benjamin, differs favorably from the symbol: if the symbol tends to generate the effect of a living, animated presence, allegory represents the very process of the body getting rid of the soul. The concept of deconstruction, as it was developed by Jacques Derrida, could equally be thought of as a delineation of a "different" metanoia of this kind—namely, as the thematization of a post-death decomposition, already anticipated in life. We are talking here about the perpetual and everlasting decay of the body, which has neither beginning nor end.

The "Muselmann," someone who has become almost a living corpse under the conditions of a concentration camp, as he is described by Giorgio Agamben in his book *Homo Sacer* (2004), is understood by the author as the embodiment of "bare life." Agamben declares the living corpse to be the carrier of true, genuine, pure life, from whose unique perspective social, "animated" life can be properly apprehended. In a similar vein, these reflections can be applied to the characters that dominate today's mass-cultural imagination, which is full of immortal bodies without souls. One has to think only of the many vampires, zombies, clones, and living machines—the miscellaneous undead—who take pride of place in today's mass culture.

But in our culture, the actual locations of physical immortality are our various archives—and in particular the museums. Works of art are the corpses of objects. In art museums, objects are kept and put on display after their death: after they have been defunctionalized, removed from the practice of life. The life of artworks in museums is a life after death, a vampiric life protected from the sunlight. At the same time, today's art museums demonstrate particularly clearly the difficulties confronting those who seek heteronoia. The aim of the European avant-gardes was and remains—even if today one

repeatedly hears that the avant-garde is no more—to demonstrate
the material, the purely corporeal, the *cadavérique*. Hand in
hand with this aim, objects become removed from the context of
their everyday use, which has allowed their pure materiality,
their corporeality—and reality of a corpse—to be overlooked.
However, the viewing of art leads repeatedly to a lively
communication with artworks—to an aesthetic experience, to
interpretation, to historicization, et cetera. Briefly: too
many souls are projected onto artworks, hindering heteronoia;
the viewer looks at the artwork from a worldly perspective,
instead of changing perspective and beginning to observe the
world from the perspective of the museum—that is, to view
the world as a corpse.

That is why contemporary art aims to make the corpse look
increasingly corpse-like—in order to make impossible further
projections of the soul onto works of art. Art today demon-
strates an increasing degree of decay and decomposition,
an increasingly radical, volatile, and transitory nature.
In the modern and contemporary art rooms of the museum,
the stages of art's development appear as stages of decay.
First, the mimetic image disintegrates—the material substance
of the work of art becomes evident. Then the body of the artwork itself begins to disintegrate. It suffers sawing, damage,
dirt, reduction to a black square or a simple cube, all of
which resist any attempt on the part of the spectator to see
other than mere material objects—corpses. Then come performances, actions, and projects, of whose corpses only some vague
material traces still remain. These are presented in installations, which, rather than being designed as complete bodies,
are arranged as accumulations of body parts and can be rear-
ranged, partially exchanged, or even completely replaced by
different body parts.

The creation of icons of a radical, *cadavérique* profanity can
of course only be successful for a short period of time: that
period during which the violence with which a specific object
was torn from the everyday still remains palpable. We know
that Duchamp's urinal will never again find its place in the
bathroom; Warhol's Campbell's Soup can will never return to
the supermarket to be purchased and consumed, and it leaves us
with a feeling of infinite sadness. In this sense, Lenin's mau-
soleum in Moscow's Red Square is particularly characteristic:
there, Lenin is put on display to prove that he is really dead
and will never arise—at least as long as his corpse remains on
view. The suspicion that resurrection is possible or might even
have already occurred can only be taken into consideration when
the corpse disappears. Lenin's corpse could thus be considered
a readymade in the tradition of Duchamp—a readymade manifesting
the finality of death.

The classical metanoia gave legitimacy to the philosophers, at least in Plato's view, to govern the polis, or the state. The Christian church has also long substantiated its claim for leadership through assertions of its ability to consider and judge finite, mortal activities on this earth from the metaperspective of the soul's immortality. Here the political dimension of the question of individual immortality and our capability for metanoia becomes very clear. In this respect, heteronoia is no exception: the heterotopian gaze is simultaneously the gaze of power. But here the philosopher becomes an artist—or, better, a museum curator. At the end of the nineteenth century, the Russian philosopher Nikolai Fedorov developed the project of the "common cause," which called upon the modern state to resurrect and make immortal, through science, all individuals who have ever lived upon the earth.[2] Fedorov used the art museum as a model for the utopian society of immortals he wanted to build. Here we have a heteronoia involving an entire society, which would transform the entire societal space into a heterotopia. The state would become a museum of its own population, and every individual would become an artwork. As the museum's administrators bear responsibility not only for the collection's inventory but also for the perfect condition of each and every artwork, sending them for restoration if they are threatened by deterioration, so the state should bear responsibility for the resurrection and afterlife of each and every individual. The state should no longer allow individuals to die in private. It ought not to allow the dead to lie in their coffins.

As Foucault famously put it, the modern state can be defined by the maxim "it makes live and lets die"—as opposed to the earlier sovereign state, which "makes die and lets live."[3] During modernity, the natural death of the individual has been considered a private affair into which, as Foucault describes it, the state declines to intervene. What is most interesting about Fedorov's project is that it doesn't consider death a private affair. Rather, Fedorov takes with full seriousness the promise of the emerging biopower—that is, the state's promise to take care of life as such; he calls upon the state to think and fulfill this promise to its logical end. Fedorov is primarily reacting to some of the contradictions inherent in the socialist teachings of the nineteenth century, which were taken up not only by himself but also by other authors of his time, in particular Dostoevsky. Socialism promised complete social justice, while simultaneously connecting this promise to the belief in progress. This belief implies that only future generations living in a fully developed, socialist society will be able to enjoy complete social justice. In contrast, previous and current generations take on a role of passive victims of progress and can expect no justice in all eternity. Therefore, future generations will be enjoying socialist justice at the cost of their cynical acceptance of an outrageous historical injustice—namely, the exclusion of all previous generations from the future society. Socialism thus functions as an exploitation of the dead for the benefit of the living—and as exploitation of those who live now for the benefit of those who will live later. The only possibility for socialism to construct a just society in the future is to aim to resurrect all those generations that created the basis for its success. Those resurrected generations will thus be able to participate in the future socialism, and the provisory discrimination of the dead for the benefit of the living will finally be eliminated. The coming society, in order to be a just one, cannot remain only contemporary. This socialism, having become completed in the future, must establish itself not only in space, but also in time, transforming the latter into eternity through technology. Before it can be considered just, a society must be not only international (that is, reaching across space) but also intergenerational (reaching across time).

Not for nothing did many Russian intellectuals and artists willingly accept Fedorov's ideas after the October Revolution. In their first manifesto in 1922, representatives of the Biocosmic-Immortalist movement, a political group with origins in Russian anarchism, wrote the following: "For us, essential and real human rights are the right of being (immortality, resurrection, rejuvenation) and the right of mobility in the cosmic space (and not the alleged rights proclaimed in the declaration of the bourgeois revolution of 1789)."[4] Thus, Aleksandr Sviatogor, one of the main proponents of the Biocosmic-Immortalist movement, considered immortality to be both the aim and the condition for the future communist society, for he believed that true social solidarity could be established solely among immortals. As long as each individual possessed a private "piece of time," actual private property could not be abolished. A total biopower, on the other hand, signified not only the collectivization of space, but also of time. Only in eternity could the conflicts between the individual and society—insolvable in real time—be successfully resolved. The goal of physical immortality was the highest goal for each individual, and only when society adopted this goal as its own would an individual remain forever loyal to society.[5]

Indisputably, among the most spectacular and far-reaching results of this program were the theories of rocket propulsion developed by Konstantin Tsiolkovsky at the same time. Tsiolkovsky actually aspired to the so-called patrification of the sky: the colonization of cosmic space by humanity's soon-to-be-immortal ancestors.[6] Later on, his research became the starting point for Soviet space travel. Another fascinating biopolitical experiment, albeit not quite so influential, was the Institute for Blood Transfusion founded and directed in the 1920s by Aleksandr Bogdanov. In his youth, Bogdanov was a close friend of Lenin's; he was also a cofounder of the intellectual-political wing of the Russian Social Democratic party, which later led to the emergence of bolshevism. In the 1920s, Bogdanov became deeply enthusiastic about blood transfusion, which he expected would achieve a deceleration, if not the total annihilation, of the aging process. He thought that blood transfusions between younger and older generations would rejuvenate the latter and simultaneously serve to balance out intergenerational solidarity. Incidentally, Bogdanov died during one of these transfusions.

For today's reader, the reports of Bogdanov's Institute for Blood Transfusion evoke first and foremost the 1897 novel *Dracula* by Bram Stoker. For example, in one purported case from Bogdanov's institute, the blood of a young female student was partially exchanged "with the blood of an older writer," the exchange from which both were alleged to have benefited equally.[7] This analogy is by no means coincidental. The society of vampires—of immortal bodies—described by Stoker is the society of a biopower par excellence. However, the novel (written, by the way, at the time that Fedorov was developing his project of the "common cause") describes the regime of the total biopower not as a utopia, but rather as an anti-utopia. And so the "human" heroes of the novel bitterly defend their right to a natural death. Their fight against the society of vampires, which establishes and guarantees physical immortality, has continued in Western mass culture ever since, although the temptations of vampiric seduction have never been completely suppressed. The rejection of physical immortality is certainly not new, to which the stories of Faust, Frankenstein, and golem well attest. Today's vampires, though, as they are depicted in books and films, are not loners. They constitute a society built not only across nations, but also across generations, a communist society of immortal bodies—in fact, resembling very much the resurrected bodies that Fedorov and Bogdanov had in mind. This is probably the very reason why such a strong resistance to this kind of society exists, as does the temptation to be part of it. To understand the radical biopolitical imagination of our times, fixated as it is on corporeal immortality, we should, it seems to me, read Fedorov, Bogdanov, and Bram Stoker simultaneously.

Notes

1.   Michel Foucault, "Des espaces autres" (1967), *Architecture-Mouvement-Continuité*, no. 5 (October 1984): 46-49.

2.   Nikolai Fedorov, "What Was Man Created For?," *The Philosophy of the Common Task: Selected Works*, trans. and ed. Elisabeth Kutaissoff and Marilyn Minto (Lausanne: Honeyglen Publishing, 1990).

3.   Michel Foucault, *Society Must Be Defended: Lectures at the Collège de France, 1975-1976*, trans. David Macey (New York: Picador, 2003), 241.

4.   "Deklarativnaia resolutsiia," *Kreatorii rossiyskikh I moskovskikh anarkhistov-biokosmitov*, no. 1 (1922): 17-18.

5.   Aleksandr Sviatogor, "Doktrina ottsov I anarkhizm-biokosmizm," *Biokosmist*, nos. 3-4 (1922): 17-18.

6.   Konstantin Tsiolkovsky, "Kosmicheskaia filosofiia" (1935), in *Tsiolokowsky: Kosmicheskaia filosofiia* (Moscow, 2001), 348-354.

7.   Alexander Bogdanov, *The Struggle for Viability: Collectivism Through Blood Exchange*, trans. and ed. Douglas W. Huestis (Tucson: Xlibris Corp., 2001).

Translated from German by Elena Sorokina and Emily Speers Mears.

A version of this essay was presented as a video lecture at Swiss Institute on April 30, 2015. This essay was originally published in *RES: Anthropology and Aesthetics*, no. 53/54 (Spring/ Autumn 2008), 345-349. A version of it was also published in Boris Groys, *Going Public* (Berlin and New York: Sternberg Press and e-flux, 2010), 152-166.

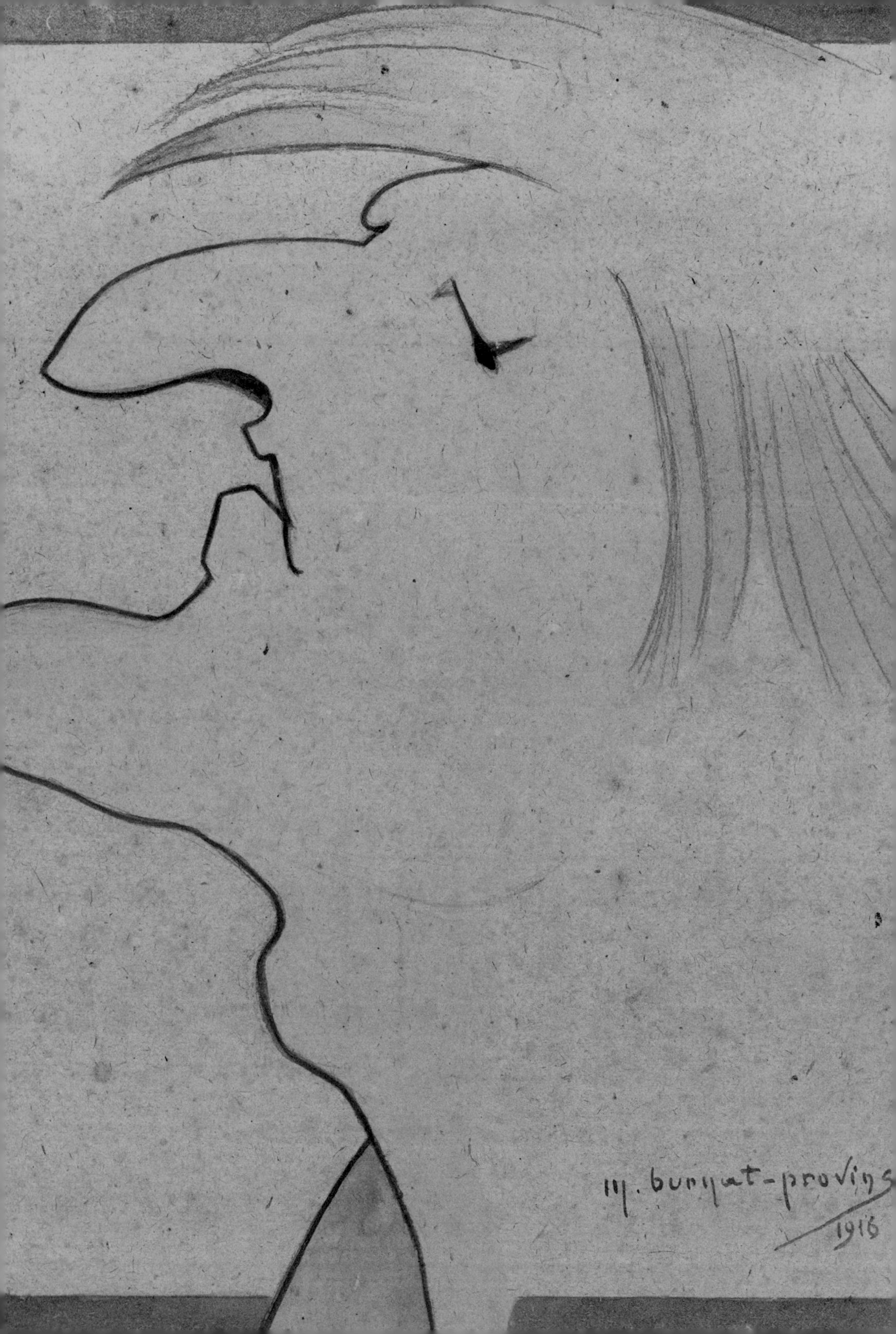
m. burnat-provins
1916

Some Unknown Portraits of Old Friends
Balthazar Lovay

She was a sacristan, actually. Truth be told, I didn't know that this job could be delegated to a woman. She was in charge of managing two chapels and one church. Since they were located in two geographically opposed neighborhoods, it was essential for her to have a flawless sense of organization and a keen knowledge of the numerous schedules of masses, prayers, weddings, and other church-related events (not to mention those of public transportation), so that each institution could welcome its worshippers in the most immaculate environment.

None of the respective parishes knew that she was involved with other dioceses. If there were schedule conflicts, or if she had to be at two different places at once, she would feign illness at one parish so that a friend could replace her, even though she was in fact officiating at another church at the same time. She had devised an ingenious system, and without realizing it she was developing a sort of asceticism, with a link neither to faith nor to religious belief, but with a quasi-spiritual value, as it required so much concentration and self-abnegation.

This layer hidden in the depths of her personality remained unknown because people knew her as the former director of a luxurious and refined swingers' club that had closed following a case of fraud, for which she had not really been responsible. Though she received a meager sum from Social Services, people knew that she lived nicely thanks to the savings she had amassed during the prosperous years preceding her trial. No one really thought that she needed to work as a sacristan to live decently.

———

Four teeth. That's all he had left. In fact, he had never really used them. He lived with his aunt, who only knew two recipes: minced sausages with potatoes mashed with a fork, and a cheese-and-mayonnaise pie. They shared an apartment in the northern part of town where the buildings were no higher than three floors. Their building only had two floors, although a small turret-like structure housing a laundry room mimicked a third one. He had collected country-rock LPs for most of his life. He had more than 10,000 of them. His musical tastes weren't all that nuanced or defined; his record collection did not express a passion for a particular genre or band, nor was it a means of socialization or even a manifestation of Diogenes syndrome. Rather, chance had decided for him when, one winter morning, one of his great-uncles, a mover who lived in an adjacent neighborhood, brought him a box of third-rate recordings. Although the box remained unopened in the hallway for months, he eventually took notice of it and soon afterward found that expanding this first batch could be a relaxing activity. From this moment on, his days were much fuller and busier than before, even if each day—in a sweeping motion of infinite repetition—was always like the previous one. His daily routine consisted of going from one café to another, where he consulted the classifieds, then to the secondhand shop to dig up wholesale deals or repossessed collections. He would come home in the evening to eat the cheese-and-mayonnaise pie that proved to be a reassuring comfort, a way of nestling in daily simplicity and repetition. The idea of getting a turntable to play his vinyl records never crossed his mind. Nevertheless, he took great care of them, sorted them, and lined them up in alphabetical order. In the end, the owner of the building donated the collection to the local library. Today, one room of the institution is named after him, although no one really knows who he was or what he did.

———

He was a former mystic who ended up adopting revolutionary ideas. He thought that in order to reach a high spiritual level, it was first necessary to destroy the established order, a key condition for the freeing of consciousness and for metaphysical renewal. He became an intensely committed anarchist and perpetrated attacks and bombings against symbols of capitalist society, which, according to him, was responsible for humankind's spiritual misery. Over a period of ten years, more than sixty people were killed in these bloody attacks. After his death, more than 1,600 drawings representing all of the stages of his ideological and spiritual journey were discovered behind a secret door. Long disdained by the spiritualists of his time, he became after his death a respected figure both for his thinking and for his graphic works, while still being reviled for his actions. Today, his works are sometimes presented within a theoretical, pedagogical, and reflective framework. Rare are the institutions that dare present his work in an autonomous manner.

———

He got arrested for having thrown cheese in an apartment hallway for about four hours.

Noon. The start of a stifling and sweltering August. He arrived from Düsseldorf, which he had left at eight o'clock in the morning in a sturdy Mercedes, the type usually driven by big industry bosses from the Ruhr area. His trunk was loaded with about 50 to 70 kilograms [110 to 154 pounds] of fireworks and light military explosives bought on the sly from a Turkish dealer at a flea market in town. Everyone, even the neighbors' children, got to work unloading and setting up this unforgettable arsenal in the field next to the house. Without even waiting for everything to be ready and secured, he lit the first firecrackers and the entire pyrotechnic show blazed, burst, exploded, gleamed, shone, and burned in total invisibility in this bright midsummer sky. Twenty minutes later, he left for the airport to catch a plane to Chicago.

———

She learned to decipher her first letters at age three. At five, she was able to read and even compose short texts of several sentences with perfect grammar and spelling. For several years, she was considered a role model to her brother, sister, and classmates. When she was about twelve, a teacher grabbed a book by the Marquis de Sade out of her backpack. Although she was able to partly understand the different and complex levels of reading that the novelist and philosopher brought forth in his text, her parents and the educational establishment scolded her for possessing such a work and closed off her bright, brilliant mind with a lid of rigorous, infantile protection. Years later, she had become a strong-willed public figure with an exceptional career as an oil broker. For two decades, her name was on everyone's lips, her face was in all the newspapers, and her involvement in an administrative council instantly raised profits for the company. Upon learning via one of the first private radios in the city that war had broken out, she sank into a deep lethargy. She came out of it little by little thanks to visions that revealed themselves to her and that she forced herself to put down on paper as small watercolor paintings. She thus illuminated hundreds of sheets with abstract compositions that are simultaneously recognizable and impenetrable, and that today have been rediscovered by professionals and the public after thirty years of a quasi-secret existence.

———

He was a far more surprising character than many people thought. He was rich and had an established career; the bulk of his fortune came from his first wife. He was a painter with undeniable critical and commercial success who had decided to live in the remote countryside to work in peace and raise his five children with his wife, his mistress, and the governesses who themselves would become his mistresses. The family lived in an astonishing neoclassical castle that he had built in less than three years, a real challenge for this time period. Although this life—if not aristocratic, then at least bourgeois—afforded him much comfort far from any difficulties, he took on a political commitment to progressive leftist forces in an important city more than 200 kilometers [124 miles] away. He often traveled to the city for business, and there, far from his castle and the bucolic countryside, he contributed to a very radical anarcho-syndicalist publication. Without really lying or hiding his two very different lives, he maintained this mildly schizophrenic existence for fifteen years. Knowing nothing of his double life, the inhabitants of the city nearly elected him governor—if not for the fascists who had succeeded in winning over his opposition. Even though he had never had to fight for his own bread or to feed his scrawny, famished children, and even if his activities might have seemed like a distractive hobby for such a person, he firmly and honestly believed in commitment.

———

His obsession with the comfort and exhilaration he felt from failure and loss was rivaled only by his obsessive desire to be the most powerful being among us. He wanted to conquer the world and truly believed it was in his power to do so. Although he saw the world in very conservative terms regarding social progress, it was his embrace of the notions of forfeiture and decrepitude that paradoxically allowed him to stay alive, to keep one foot in the real world and partake in everyday life. In addition to using these ideas as an introspective tool, he also implemented them in his business. A number of the products that earned him his fortune possess in their very DNA a symbolism of debacle and decay—a manner in which to confront one's destiny and shake up the stability of certainties. Such an approach to life had led to his current state, a condition of constant urgency whose complexity no one could truly grasp.

Translated from French by Diane Gerspacher.

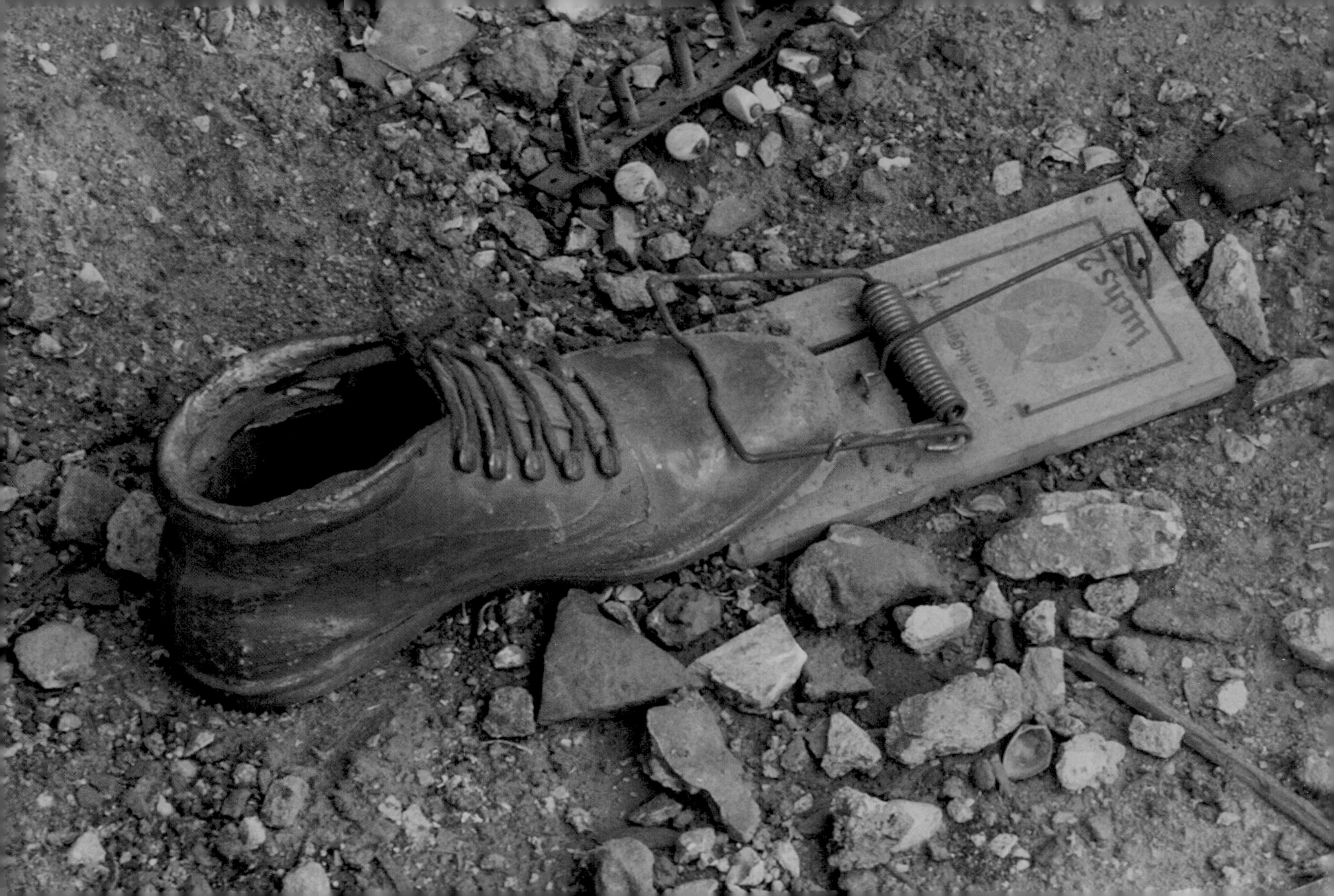
luchs 2
Made in W. Germany

When Exhibitions Become Form:
On the History of the Artist as Curator
Elena Filipovic

Caveat lector. This essay's subtitle is a false lead. A history of the artist as curator remains to be fully written.[1] Publications on the museum, exhibition practices, and even star curators have, in recent years, grown into a veritable cottage industry, with entire bookshelves devoted to the subjects, even though a mere two decades ago one would have been hard-pressed to find more than a single volume about them.[2] In the context of long-sustained and venerable art historical scholarship, the history of the exhibition remains a still-nascent, if rapidly expanding, field. Curator figures, from Harald Szeemann and Seth Siegelaub to Lucy Lippard, overshadow that field—their projects, practices, and words garnering significant attention. As I write this, the practice of reconstructing an exhibition, a relatively rare curatorial act before now, has reached new heights with the re-creation of über-curator Szeemann's landmark 1969 exhibition *When Attitudes Become Form*, which restages the seminal show almost work by work, square meter by square meter.[3] Against this background, one must wonder: why have exhibitions by artists remained so relatively impervious to historicization?

We know some of the fabulous stories, like the one about Gustave Courbet setting up shop across the way from the 1855 Salon in Paris. His rogue pavilion aimed to present his work differently and better, he claimed, than the French state would have in its crammed annual exhibition, where paintings were stacked to the ceiling with apparent disregard for the integrity of the works on show. The Salon officials had rejected the artist's major works from the period, including *The Artist's Studio* (1854-55) and *A Burial at Ornans* (1849-50), so his entrepreneurial one-man show (something unheard of in its day) would, he imagined, be not only a fitting riposte, but also a revenge on the exhibition conventions favored by the Salon. One can picture him, realist painting's master craftsman, peddling photographic reproductions of his paintings and charging for admission as well as for the checking of canes and umbrellas in order to pay for the affair.[4] In a time long before the advent of the fully professionalized species known as the "curator," an artist was endeavoring, on his own, to choose the location, organize the scenography, make the selection of artworks to be featured, and even devise the financing scheme—all so that he might better determine the conditions of his work's reception. Together with the twentieth century, even more such seeming anomalies arrived: artists who not only quietly made discrete objects in their studios but took into their own hands the very apparatus of presentation and dissemination of the work they had produced—and often that of other artists as well.

The annals of art history are full of such anecdotes, although they sit almost without exception on the periphery of official narratives. The reasons for this are perhaps no mystery: despite its fundamental importance as a primary context through which art is first made public, circulated, seen, and discussed, the exhibition has long been considered an ambiguous object of study at best, partly due to the tenuousness of the exhibition's—*any* exhibition's—ontological ground, no matter who curated it. Neither a stable, immutable, collectible thing (the usual stuff of art history), nor a clear product of any single hand (being, as they are, determined as much by the artist-made objects they comprise as by the curator who organizes said objects); decidedly not autonomous; often deemed "merely" a frame; and irrevocably tied to the mundane pragmatics of administration (thus supposedly less "pure" and "creative" than an artwork): these are some of the reasons that might explain why exhibition history, in general, took so long to gain traction as a bona fide object of study. Yet why the peculiar and specific genus that is the artist-curated exhibition has taken even longer to be theorized requires another explanation.

Any explanation would surely be related to the ontological impurity of exhibitions in the wider sense, but artist-curated examples arguably further exacerbate the exhibition's precarious nature, sitting uncomfortably close to artistic work, and yet still evidently not quite qualifying as artworks. Even if they are the product of an artist or artist collective, artist-curated exhibitions cannot be thought of through the romantic idea of the artist as individual producer of immutable objects that follow a progressive, evolutive development of forms classifiable according to artistic movement, style, or "turn." Neither is it clear how to consider them in relation to an artistic oeuvre. (Is an artist-curated exhibition, for instance, entered into an artist's catalogue raisonné? Does it get listed in the artist's curriculum vitae along with other group exhibitions? Or rather with the solo shows?) Nor is it apparent whether they can be usefully compared (as artworks are) in discussions regarding the development of parallel artistic oeuvres or movements.

Speaking of exhibition history in general, the writer and curator Simon Sheikh raised the following question: "What does

it mean to shift attention from objects to exhibitions? . . .
We have to ask ourselves not only what a history of exhibitions
can tell us about art but also what a history of exhibitions
will tell us about history, how it is written and read, rewritten
and reread."[5] In response, he advanced the following proposition:
if a history of exhibitions were to be written, it should perhaps
be based on the historian Reinhart Koselleck's notion of "conceptual history"—in other words, a history examined not through
stylistic or chronological devices, but instead through the
(materially embodied) concepts and ideas that presumably under-
pin the exhibitions in question.[6] Sheikh suggests, for example,
"democracy," "the state," "freedom," and "progress" as such
possible categories. Although provocative, it is not clear what
such a conceptual history of exhibitions would look like, particularly given the profoundly ambiguous nature of the concepts
he suggests, nor whether such a methodology could adequately
address the history of that complex and labile object that is
the exhibition. Yet to Sheikh's compelling set of questions one
could add: Once we have written that history, how do we attend
to the specific genus that is the artist-curated exhibition?
What can it tell us about history, art history, *and* exhibition
history—about how these are written and read, rewritten and reread?

After all, there is the question of how to contextualize artist-
curated exhibitions. Should their narration follow (like most
art history courses being taught even today) a linear, chronological, even progressive direction (think of Alfred H. Barr,
Jr.'s famous flow chart), going from, say, Courbet to Mark
Leckey? Or, instead, might one think in terms of typologies
rather than chronology (or style or movement)?[7] Such typologies
could include solo projects as exhibitions (Claes Oldenburg's
The Store, 1961; Marcel Broodthaers's *Département des Aigles*,
1968-72); political-activist exhibitions (Group Material's
AIDS Timeline, 1989; Alice Creischer, Andreas Siekmann, and
Max Jorge Hinderer's *The Potosí Principle*, 2010); the rearrang-
ing of museum or other collections in, and as, exhibitions
(Andy Warhol's *Raid the Icebox*, 1969; Fred Wilson's *Mining
the Museum*, 1992); exhibitions as sensorial experiences (Yves
Klein's *Le Vide*, 1958; David Hammons's *Concerto in Black and
Blue*, 2002); and so on. Still, maybe the overarching problem
with any of these possible organizational principles is that
they fail to address the shared condition of so many of these
artist-curated exhibitions—namely, that their aims, methods,
structures, and modes of address undermine, or even denature,
established ideas of the exhibition.

Peruse Bruce Altshuler's formidable two-volume work *From
Salon to Biennial* and *Biennials and Beyond*, both subtitled
Exhibitions that Made Art History.[8] Some of the exhibitions
he features include the first Blaue Reiter exhibition, Moderne

Galerie Thannhauser, Munich, 1911; the Armory Show, New York, 1913; *Cubism and Abstract Art*, Museum of Modern Art, New York, 1936; *The New American Painting*, Tate, London, 1959; *Primary Structures*, the Jewish Museum, New York, 1966; *Magiciens de la Terre*, Centre Pompidou, Paris, 1989; and documenta 11, Kassel, 2002. There is no doubt that any and all of these merit inclusion in the history of exhibitions if for no other reason than because they introduced new art to a public. *Cubism and Abstract Art*, for example, brought together works by those eponymous movements for the first time in 1936; *Primary Structures* gathered in an institutional setting the kind of objects that would later be grouped under minimalism for the first time in 1966; *Magiciens de la Terre* challenged Western hegemonies by showing the first truly "global" panorama of art in 1989; and so on. Whatever can be said about these indeed important exhibitions that, as Altshuler suggests, "*made* art history," they were classical in many senses of the word.[9] In most cases, they simply brought the "new" into a space that remained unaltered by the confrontation, and few of them fundamentally or radically troubled the conventions, structures, and protocols of the exhibition as *form*.

Thus, rather than an exhibition whose author is simply not a curator, the very nature of what goes under the name "exhibition" might be entirely distinct from a "professionally" curated example. If it is easy to see that artist-curated exhibitions can trouble our very understanding of such notions as "artistic autonomy," "authorship," "artwork," and "artistic oeuvre," what might be less evident is that they also complicate what might count as an "exhibition." Many artist-curated exhibitions—perhaps the most striking and influential of the genre—are the result of artists treating the exhibition as an artistic medium in its own right, an *articulation of form*. In the process, they often disown or dismantle the very idea of the "exhibition" as it is conventionally thought, putting its genre, category, format, or protocols at stake and thus entirely shifting the terms of what an exhibition could be. Courbet's example suggests that the impulse among artists to take the organization of exhibitions into their own hands already existed in the late nineteenth century, yet it was for the avant-gardes of the early twentieth century to further develop the potentials of the exhibition as medium. And, following them, a postwar generation of artists finally so radically tackled the form that they fundamentally transformed the shape of exhibitions thereafter—not only those curated by artists, but also those generated by professional curators.

In order to better understand how artists approached the genre throughout the twentieth and twenty-first centuries, an examination of the case of Marcel Duchamp provides an interesting, pioneering example. While he is most lauded for the provocation of claiming a store-bought object as art, his lifelong role as curator was arguably no less radical or influential a gesture. Dorothea von Hantelmann credits Duchamp with inaugurating what she calls "the curatorial paradigm," arguing that: "In the field of art it was Marcel Duchamp who anticipated, paradigmatically performed, and articulated" a new archetype of creativity. In her view, it was his *choice* (which is what she considers *curatorial*) that allowed the readymade to mark "the transition of a production-oriented society to a selection-oriented society."[10]

Von Hantelmann goes on to state: "Duchamp turned the act of choosing into a new paradigm of creativity. Or, rather, he sharpened a practice that has always existed into something like a paradigm." That Duchamp inaugurated a curatorial paradigm is quite right, although I would argue that it is *not* at all because of his "choice" or "selection" with regard to the readymade (nor do I imagine the curator primarily a "selector" of things). Rather, Duchamp inaugurated a curatorial paradigm through his understanding of the exhibition as a means of interrogation, a tool by which to critically question the limits of both the (art) object and its institutions, all of which importantly determined the fate of his readymade even more than his mere selection did.[11]

Although the profession of the "curator" was hardly very defined or prevalent when Duchamp first began to adopt curatorial operations as part of his artistic practice, and he would never explicitly use the term to describe himself, the notion progressively became concretized in the half-century during which he worked, solidifying into its present-day sense, describing an art professional attending to the manifold tasks connected to the caretaking of art and its public exhibition.[12] Still, the "curator," no matter how one defined that role specifically, had aims and responsibilities quite distinct from that of the artist, and vice versa, making it all the more unusual that Duchamp so frequently and insistently engaged in the tasks associated with curatorial work. More than occasional occupations or undertakings ancillary to the "actual" work of the artist and the artwork, Duchamp arguably made "curatorial" tasks a veritable lifework and the pivotal catalyst through which to understand and expose the artwork as such.[13] Indeed, through Duchamp's deep preoccupation with the institutional sites, mechanisms, and conventions that accompany and ostensibly lie outside of the artwork, he radically shifted both the exhibition's and the artwork's terms (and not solely, as has been so long thought, through an act of artistic fiat—either "invention," "declaration," or "selection"—that transformed a urinal into *Fountain*).

One could cite his early relationship to exhibitions as a
prelude to his later, actual curating: for instance, in 1916,
in response to an eager gallerist's request to feature one
of his paintings in a group show, he insisted on including two
of his readymades as well—making it their first public appearance in an exhibition. He placed the everyday objects without
fanfare or indication in the coat-check area of the gallery
(with no label, no pedestal, no special lighting, and no
discussion about them), and they—perhaps unsurprisingly—went
totally unnoticed.[14] Duchamp was not in any way the curator
here, but his orchestration of the exercise seems to treat the
exhibition not only as a locale for the presentation of things
but also as a site of inquiry, a testing ground from which the
artist might have learned that an object perhaps only appears
as a work of art under certain conditions, one of which is to
be explicitly on *exhibit*, with all the protocol this entails.
After this incident, Duchamp would repeatedly and insistently
be involved in curating exhibitions, recognizing that the
discursive and institutional apparatuses around the artwork
could be used, experimented with, rethought. Ultimately, as his
exhibitions from the 1930s until the end of his life reveal,
he rendered the exhibition utterly unlike the showplaces of
artifacts hung more or less high on the wall that the museum
at the time treated them as.

Only one year later, in 1917, a time before the term "curator"
was widely used, let alone before the idea of an artist-curator
had any currency, Duchamp took on the role of president of
the "hanging committee" for the inaugural exhibition of the
Society of Independent Artists in New York.[15] In that capacity,
he devised a curious system for the arrangement of the show,
proposing to hang the artworks not according to school, style,
or chronology, but alphabetically and, according to chance,
beginning the exhibition with the first letter selected from
a hat—thereby ensuring absolutely no favoritism while defy-
ing every known system according to which shows were typically
organized. Arguably, it was precisely because he was president
of the hanging committee that he made sure that another gesture
he performed would be anonymous: he pseudonymously submitted a
store-bought piece of porcelain plumbing entitled *Fountain* to
the exhibition. The urinal, signed "R. Mutt 1917," was, as the
now-famous story goes, rejected before being lost or destroyed
(no one quite knows which).[16] Few had any idea that a certain
Marcel Duchamp was behind *Fountain*; not even some of his clos-
est friends and patrons knew, and the artist didn't publicly
mention his connection to the object for decades.[17] As far as
von Hantelmann's idea of curatorial paradigms go, the urinal
may have been an artwork selected, but in 1917 it had not been
shown or noticed, and it had decidedly not entered into history. It might as well have never existed.[18]

When Duchamp did finally reveal his connection to *Fountain*—which is to say, when he began several decades later to construct a public history for an object that by that point no longer existed and one that had, moreover, made no impact while it did exist—his revelation was entirely bound up with his thinking about exhibitions, art institutions, and their administration of what counts as "Art." The "invention" of the readymade needed to be curated; in other words, it required a public exhibition, which it finally got in Duchamp's creation of an exhibition in a suitcase, *Boîte-en-valise* (Box in a Valise, 1938-42). The artist constructed the miniature portable exhibition for his *Fountain* (along with reproductions of sixty-eight other artworks) at the exact moment that he was preparing the first of what would be a series of elaborate exhibitions with the surrealists for which he was the curator (or, the "generator-arbitrator," in the surrealists' and his idiosyncratic terminology). He would act in that role again and again over his lifetime: first in 1938, then in 1942, 1947, 1959, and 1960. In other words, Duchamp's investigations into the enunciative capacity and authoritative functioning of the full-sized exhibition is inseparable from his creation of a miniature version of a retrospective exhibition that allowed him to play, literally, the museum's game on his own terms. On the other hand, with flashlights as exhibition lighting, suspended coal bags as a ceiling, and department-store revolving doors as supports for paintings (as in the *Exposition international du surréalisme* [International Surrealist Exhibition] in 1938), or with artworks strung among a web of several miles of ordinary string that obstructed passage and vision (as for the *First Papers of Surrealism* exhibition in 1942), to name just two examples, his exhibitions were, in each case, radical reimaginings of the conventions of display that proved immensely influential to the generations of artists that came after him.

Indeed there are numerous examples of artists who, each in their own way, subsequently took up the practice of exhibition-making as a critical medium. In the postwar period, Richard Hamilton and Victor Pasmore's programmatically titled *an Exhibit* of 1957 is of emblematic dimensions.[19] Comprised of variously colored acrylic sheets differing in their degree of transparency, strung from the ceiling and placed at right angles to each other, the exhibition appeared as a maze-like spatial structure within which spectators could move about. It was an exhibition with "no images," which in the artists' minds meant no artworks as such, and, in Hamilton's words, "no subject, no theme other than itself," which is to say, nearly none of the primary elements that would make an exhibition an exhibition. Instead, as Hamilton added, "it was self-referential,"[20] and, explaining his intentions further, "I wanted to . . . make the exhibition into an art form in its own right—*an exhibition about*

an exhibition" (italics mine).[21] In the process, the artists made
a display of *display*. As both the content and driving methodology of the exhibition, "display" became a material surface
and catalyst for visual and spatial experience. Hamilton and
Pasmore's gesture of withdrawal—"un-exhibiting" as a mode of
exhibiting—along with similarly radical methodologies advanced
in a number of other artist-curated exhibitions that would
follow in *an Exhibit*'s wake, pursued the radical reversal
of the art exhibition's usual mandate: questioning, probing,
reimagining what the content and the terms of display for exhibitions could be.

Less than a year later, for his exhibition *Le Vide* (The Void),
Yves Klein painted the whole interior of a Parisian art gallery
exhibition space white, removing all of the usual, recognizable
"content" from the space. It was not just a gallery emptied
or simply repainted: the very whiteness that was the signature
of the modern white cube was rendered an extreme of itself.
Whiter than white, Klein's careful paint job combined several
coats of pure white lithopone pigment blended with his own
special varnish of alcohol, acetone, and vinyl resin.[22] As he
later recounted:

> The object of this endeavor: to create, establish, and
> present to the public a palpable pictorial state in the
> limits of a picture gallery. In other words, the creation
> of an ambience, a genuine pictorial climate, and, there-
> fore, an invisible one. This invisible pictorial state
> within the gallery space should be so present and endowed
> with autonomous life that it should literally be what has
> hitherto been regarded as the best overall definition of
> painting: radiance.[23]

The exhibition opening was a willfully provocative, decidedly
staged affair. Many of the conventions of the art exhibition
were used, but also exaggerated: specially printed invitation
cards (3,500—a considerable number for a gallery show at the
time), a commissioned text by a critic, an entrance fee (unheard
of in commercial galleries but common in museums), an opening
speech, drinks for the occasion (special blue cocktails),and
hired guards out front (two mounted Republican guards, no
less). And when Klein discovered a young man playfully drawing
on his freshly painted gallery wall, he promptly called secu-
rity and had him thrown out. In other words, the space operated
according to many of the rules and institutional policies that
would typically characterize an exhibition, except for the
radical evacuation of the exhibition's conventional raison
d'être: anything that might be mistaken for an artwork on
exhibit was absent.

A few years later, in December 1966, Mel Bochner, then a young instructor at the School of Visual Arts in New York, placed four identical ring binders—each with one hundred copies of studio notes, working drawings, and diagrams collected and xeroxed by the artist—on pedestals in the school's gallery for its winter show. He entitled it *Working Drawings and Other Visible Things on Paper Not Necessarily Meant to Be Viewed as Art*.[24] Each binder contains photocopies of preparatory drawings for artists' projects: Dan Flavin's proposals for his light installations, Sol LeWitt's sketches of white lattices, Eva Hesse's numerical progressions, Carl Andre's studies for poetry, and Donald Judd's work plans (including even a bill for Judd's fabrication costs), as well as the technical drawing of the Xerox machine used to make the copies included in the binders. As an exhibition, *Working Drawings* deployed some of the most recognizable conventions of the exhibition at the time—a white-cube space, pristine display conditions, pedestals—but used them in order to undermine some of the very pillars of the exhibition by operating according to minimal and conceptual paradigms instead of presenting anything that would have looked like bona fide art at the time. *Working Drawings* "dematerialized" the auratic, visual artwork into a reproducible idea, a notion that became a hallmark of late-1960s conceptualism. By displaying a reproducible document that seemed like a catalogue with all the markers of an artwork on exhibition, Bochner not only prioritized what Siegelaub would later call "secondary" over "primary" information, but he actually made a show of it. It is fitting, perhaps, that it is said that when the Museum of Modern Art rejected Bochner's offer to donate the binders to the museum's collection as artworks (they were the product, after all, of artists' generative processes) and instead only agreed to accept them as a potential donation to the museum's library, Bochner refused. Although the story is perhaps apocryphal, the fact that it still circulates is telling. It is about a museum (as museums are wont to do) attempting to defend the idea of the singular work of art against the perceived threat of "the reproduction." For Bochner, however, *Working Drawings* purposefully destabilized hierarchies between originality and reproduction as much as it did between exhibition and artwork.

On the other side of the globe, a series of events and exhibitions by a group of young Argentine artists from Buenos Aires and Rosario called the Experimental Art Cycle took place in 1968. Their activities would lead to the conception of a large activist research, information, and exhibition campaign, *Tucumán Arde* (Tucumán Burns), held later that year.[25] As part of the cycle of events that led to *Tucumán Arde*, the artist Graciela Carnevale opened her *Acción del Encierro* (Confinement Action) in an empty Rosario storefront gallery whose windows had been papered over by the artist. The event consisted of her locking up attendees to the opening for more than an hour. Guests (or "prisoners," as the artist later referred to them) only afterward realized that their sequestration in the empty exhibition space (and the resultant confusion, fear, paranoia, and eventual escape) *was* the exhibition itself; the confinement made them, as the artist recounts, "obliged, violently, to participate"—an effect partially thwarted by a passerby who saw the desperate, incarcerated crowd (which by this point had peeled off the posters covering the window) and broke the glass to let them out.[26] Once outside of the exhibition context, and just before the police brought the exhibition-action to an abrupt end, the audience was given a photocopied statement that drew a parallel between their experience and the abuses perpetrated by the Argentine military dictatorship on a daily basis. Although *Acción del Encierro* was as much an activist performance as an exhibition, it is relevant that Carnevale specifically chose the medium and format of the exhibition as a means of staging her own version of aesthetic withdrawal, countering the expectations of the artwork and its normative, spectacular display.

An altogether different sort of refusal to deliver an exhibition of artworks (or, in this case, the solo show that the original invitation to the artist specified) was Martha Rosler's 1989 *If You Lived Here . . .* held at the Dia Art Foundation, New York.[27] Part artist research project, part curated group exhibition (itself made up of three exhibition cycles, four public meetings, and numerous accompanying events), it offered a makeshift, disorderly mix of art and non-art items (charts, graphs, maps, newspaper clippings) by known and less-known artists and non-artists alike, about homelessness, housing injustices in New York, and the conditions that made such things possible. Delivering an implicit critique of the host institution, located in the then-flourishing art market district in SoHo, the project connected its immediate exhibition surroundings to broader systems that made homelessness and human precarity thrive (gentrification, corruption, complicity, rampant capitalism). Practically speaking, this was an exhibition space transformed into a town hall for meetings, providing a place for discussion, research, and information spreading, but also cooking and sleeping (with seating and makeshift shelter included). It was a place to instill activism, communal participation, and engagement. It looked and operated little like a typical art exhibition, and its reception, both by its host institution and by the local press, revealed the difficulty with which it was recognized as an exhibition at all (rather than, say, social activism). Nevertheless, through it, Rosler inspired a whole generation of artists—from Liam Gillick to Rirkrit Tiravanija—and participatory practices in art, but she also significantly influenced what went on to become called the "discursive exhibition," a pedagogic, activist turn in art that used the exhibition as a privileged public forum.

Still other examples offering altogether different responses to the question of what might constitute an exhibition could be cited, such as David Hammons's unannounced 1994 exhibition at Knobkerry, a Tribeca shop for Asian and African objects, in which items by Hammons and the shop's regular offerings were mixed with little indication, through presentation or price, as to their differing status. Throughout the shop, tongue-in-cheek, typically Hammons-like combinations could be found, such as deflated basketballs stuffed into the shop's own terra-cotta vases, cigarette butts attached to its hanging Persian carpets, or black-eyed peas laid out inside its miniature, trinket temples. A single, small, handwritten sign sat near one such readymade ensemble, telling visitors (if they noticed or cared): "Works by David Hammons Now On Exhibit."[28] Or there is Lucy McKenzie and Paulina Olowska's *Nova Popularna* (2003), an exhibition that took the form of a temporary illegal speakeasy in Warsaw. Taking over a space loaded with historical resonance as the site of avant-garde happenings in previous decades, the duo of artists designed their own brand of vernacular or "new popular" scenography (from the bar and curtains to their own uniforms, as the locale's barmaids) as the backdrop against which they presented a rotating array of artworks, performances, concerts, and other events.[29] One could name many more—indeed, the list of artist-curated exhibitions is long, and takes us from Judy Chicago and Miriam Schapiro with the CalArts Feminist Art Program's *Womanhouse* (1971) to Goshka Macuga's *Cave* (1999); from Thomas Hirschhorn's *Musée Precaire* (2004) to Willem de Rooij's *Intolerance* (2011); and from Philippe Thomas's *Feux Pâles* (1990) to Mark Leckey's *The Universal Addressability of Dumb Things* (2013), proving that artists have, from the postwar period to the present, found the exhibition an incredibly potent site of intervention.

One cannot say that every exhibition organized by an artist explicitly seeks to shift the terms of the exhibition as such; some have been, more than anything else, about expressing an artist's particular and unusual grounds for selection while the classical format for presentation remained stalwartly in place; and there are, conversely, a number of exhibitions made by "professional" curators (or, at least, non-artists), who, for their part, have managed to accomplish that task of reimagining the form of the exhibition (think of Lippard's various "numbers" shows [1969-74], Siegelaub's *Xerox Book* [1968], Gerry Schum's *Television Exhibitions* I and II [1969-70], and Jean-François Lyotard and Thierry Chaput's *Les Immatériaux* [1985]). These cases can be attributed to the curator endeavoring to find an exhibition form that would respond to the nature of the work being shown, or to the fact that the curator allowed the artists, while not taking on the role of the curator per se, to have a hand in determining the exhibition. Professional curators have certainly sometimes been inspired by artist-curated exhibitions and have felt challenged to rethink the exhibition's form as a result. In other words, there are no hard and fast rules that distinguish the categories I deploy in order to facilitate a discussion of the subject. Things *are* slippery. Nevertheless, this larger project of looking at the artist as curator aims to address what has been the signal of many artist-curated shows: a gauntlet thrown down to the idea of the exhibition as a neutral arrangement of artworks in a given space and time, for didactic or spectacular display.

However much this project might seem to unify the specific genre that is the artist-curated exhibition, it does not suggest a sameness or uniformity to artists' approaches. The examples suggest that the premises that quietly support and perpetuate the most conventional notions of the "exhibition" have long been undermined by artistic practice. And while artist-curated initiatives remain relatively understudied, they raise the thorny issues mentioned earlier, among them questions regarding the limits of the artwork (where does an artwork end and its context begin?), the status of the exhibition (should an exhibition curated by an artist be considered an artwork? How is it to be evaluated in relation to an artist's oeuvre?), and so on. As such, this project is less about constructing a canon of "landmark" exhibitions (although this is *also* an attempt to understand what the terms and perils of that could be). It is instead more about beginning to imagine possible languages, tools, and methodologies for looking at, and talking about, how a certain kind of exhibition-making advanced by artists can be studied today—alongside, but also perhaps differently from, the vast expanse of exhibitions writ large.

The Artist as Curator's ambition is manifold, but it is decidedly not meant to be a rehearsal of the mythos of the curator, whether artist or not. Rather, it is an attempt to acknowledge the critical agency of operations and activities that are taken up by artists but that might not seem "artistic" in the most traditional sense. These activities reveal an acute understanding on the part of artists regarding the exhibition's latent potential as a form to be pressed, challenged, and even undone. For the crucial task of a history of artist-curated exhibitions is to attend to the particularities not only of what was shown, but also to the form the exhibitions assumed. That form may or may not be considered an artwork, or even an exhibition, but the cases explored in this project will ask us to fundamentally reconsider what an artwork or an exhibition is—or could be.

Notes

1. Occasional references to artist-curated exhibitions appear in broader exhibition histories (Brian O'Doherty's *Inside the White Cube: The Ideology of the Gallery Space* and Bruce Altshuler's *The Avant-Garde in Exhibition: New Art in the 20th Century* offer rare, early exceptions that give significant attention to the artist-curated exhibition), and there are a handful of essays, each devoted to a single artist-curated exhibition, and even a few articles on the phenomenon of the artist as curator (on all accounts, see the "Select Bibliography on Curators, Curating, and Exhibition Histories" in this volume). But, surprisingly, there exists no comprehensive study surveying artist-curated exhibitions, nor any serious attempt to theorize the specificity of these exhibitions. Moreover, artist-curated exhibitions often get left out of larger art histories that still frequently favor discussions of autonomous objects.

2. See the "Select Bibliography" in this volume for a panoramic overview of the subject.

3. The reconstruction of historic exhibitions is not new, but the Prada Foundation's impressive recent efforts toward meticulously researching and reconstructing *When Attitudes Become Form* is both unparalleled and indicative of how woefully limited such reconstructions inevitably are. See the remarkable publication edited by Germano Celant and Chiara Costa, *When Attitudes Become Form: Bern 1969/Venice 2013* (Milan: Fondazione Prada, 2013).

4. See Patricia Mainardi, "Courbet's Exhibitionism," *Gazette des Beaux-Arts* 118 (December 1991): 253-266.

5. Simon Sheikh, "A Conceptual History of Exhibition-Making" (paper presented at Former West Conference, BAK, Utrecht, November 7, 2009).

6. Reinhart Koselleck, *The Practice of Conceptual History: Timing History, Spacing Concepts* (Stanford, CA: Stanford University Press, 2002).

7. See Pablo Lafuente's suggestion of typologies as a way to historicize post-1989 exhibitions as articulated in his "Exhibition Typologies Post-1989" (paper presented at Former West Conference, BAK, Utrecht, November 7, 2009).

8. See Bruce Altshuler, *From Salon to Biennial: Exhibitions That Made Art History, Volume 1: 1863-1959* (London: Phaidon, 2008) and *Biennials and Beyond: Exhibitions That Made Art History, 1962-2002* (London: Phaidon, 2013).

9. The ambiguity of the phrase "exhibitions that made art history" seems willful: it suggests either "shows that made it into art history" or "shows that made art history what it is today"—or both.

10. Dorothea von Hantelmann, "The Curatorial Paradigm," *The Exhibitionist* 4 (June 2011): 11-12.

11. The discussion of Duchamp's role as curator draws from my doctoral dissertation, *The Apparently Marginal Activities of Marcel Duchamp* (Princeton University, 2013).

12. In the 1920s, and parallel with the development of museums and public collections devoted to modern art, several important examples of museum director-curators emerged, including Alexander Dorner in Europe and Alfred H. Barr, Jr. in the United States, each of whom helped forge a model for what the modern curator could be. For more on the development of the notions of curator, exhibition, and museum in the modern period, see the "Select Bibliography" in this volume.

13. It was arguably Duchamp's pioneering stance that set the foundation for subsequent generations to develop what came to be called conceptual art's "aesthetics of administration" (to use Benjamin Buchloh's formulation) and institutional critique, for which curatorial and administrative tasks were a central part of artistic labor. See Benjamin Buchloh, "Conceptual Art 1962-1969: From the Aesthetic of Administration to the Critique of Institutions," *October* 55 (Winter 1990): 105-143.

14. See Thierry de Duve, *Kant After Duchamp* (Cambridge, MA: MIT Press, 1996), 102; and Bernard Marcadé, "Concept of Nothing," in *Voids* (Zürich/Paris: JRP Ringier/Centre Pompidou, 2009), 236.

15. For the Independents exhibition, there was specifically not supposed to be a "selection;" it was open to all comers, yet the president of the hanging committee was pretty much as close as one can get to the "curator" in our contemporary sense.

16. No matter that the exhibition claimed to have "no jury and no prizes" and that anyone who paid the $6 submission fee, as R. Mutt had, was supposed to be allowed to exhibit. A urinal revealed the exhibition's pretense of undogmatic inclusiveness to be, quite simply, a lie. Censored from the catalogue and the show, it was apparently hidden behind a wall partition where the public would not see it. And it was, so at least one story goes, lost almost as quickly as it had been chosen from among the lavatory supplies at the J. L. Mott ironwork and appliance showroom. For a collection of the most extensive research on the different accounts of *Fountain*, see William Camfield, *Marcel Duchamp/Fountain* (Houston: Menil Collection, Houston Fine Arts Press, 1989).

17. "For a period of thirty years nobody talked about them [the readymades], and neither did I," Duchamp later admitted in "Marcel Duchamp Talking about Readymades," interview by Philippe Collin, June 21, 1967. Reprinted in Harald Szeemann, ed., *Marcel Duchamp* (Ostfildern: Hatje Cantz, 2002), 40.

18. This fact cannot be overemphasized, since so many of the art historical references to the urinal as the seminal example of Duchampian iconoclasm fail to take adequate note of its lack of publicness at the time. They treat *Fountain* as if it were, already in 1917, the art-historical icon that it is today and as if one can properly speak of it without considering the fundamental role that its documentation, administration, and (delayed) representation in an exhibition (which is to say, its curation) has had on its contemporary interpretation.

19. See Isabelle Moffat, "Richard Hamilton and Victor Pasmore, *an Exhibit*, 1957," *Mousse* 42, no. 1 (August 2015), http://moussemagazine.it/taacl-b/.

20. "Pop Daddy: An Interview with Richard Hamilton by Hans Ulrich Obrist," *Tate Magazine* (March/April 2003), http://www.tate.org.uk/context-comment/articles/pop-daddy-richard-hamilton-early-exhibition.

21. Richard Hamilton, quoted in *Fifty Years of the Future: A Chronicle of the Institute of Contemporary Arts* (London: Institute of Contemporary Arts, 1998), http://www.helpmego.to/ica/OldWEBSITE/history/50years.pdf. See also Richard Hamilton, *Collected Words, 1953-82* (London: Thames & Hudson, 1982).

22. See Sidra Stich's descriptions of Klein's process in *Yves Klein* (London: Hayward Gallery, 1995), 135.

23. Yves Klein, "Le Vide Performance (The Void)" (lecture, Sorbonne, Paris, 1959). Translated and reprinted in *Yves Klein 1928-1962: A Retrospective* (Houston: Institute for the Arts, Rice University, 1982). See online at http://web.tiscali.it/nouveaurealisme/ENG/klein5.htm.

24. See James Meyer, "Mel Bochner, *Working Drawings And Other Visible Things On Paper Not Necessarily Meant To Be Viewed As Art*, 1966," *Mousse* 47, no. 6 (2015). Revised version of "The Second Degree: Working Drawings and Other Visible Things on Paper Not Necessarily Meant to Be Viewed as Art," in *Conceptual Art: Theory, Myth, and Practice*, ed. Michael Corris (New York: Cambridge University Press, 2004).

25. See Ana Longoni, "Avant-Garde Argentinian Visual Artists Group, *Tucumán Burns*, 1968," *Mousse* 43, no. 2 (2015). See also Longoni and Mariano Mestman, *Del Di Tella a "Tucumán Arde:" Vanguardia artística y política en el '68 argentino* (Buenos Aires: El Cielo por Asalto, 2000).

26. Graciela Carnevale's artist statement reads: "The work consists of first preparing a
    totally empty room, with totally empty walls. One of the walls, which was made of glass,
    had to be covered in order to achieve a suitably neutral space for the work to take place.
    In this room the participating audience, which has come together by chance for the opening,
    has been locked in. The door has been hermetically closed without the audience being aware
    of it. I have taken prisoners. The point is to allow people to enter and to prevent them
    from leaving. Here the work comes into being and these people are the actors. There is no
    possibility of escape, in fact the spectators have no choice; they are obliged, violently,
    to participate. Their positive or negative reaction is always a form of participation."
    Graciela Carnevale, "El encierro—Project for the Experimental Art Series," *Re.act
    Feminism*, accessed November 2013, http://www.reactfeminism.org/entry.php?l=1b&id=27&e=a.
27. See Nina Möntmann, "(Under) Privileged Spaces: On Martha Rosler's 'If You Lived
    Here . . . ,'" *e-flux journal* 9 (October 2009), http://www.e-flux.com/journal/
    underprivileged-spaces-on-martha-rosler's-"if-you-lived-here-"/.
28. See my forthcoming essay on the subject of *Untitled (Knobkerry)* as part of this series.
29. See Adam Szymczyk's forthcoming essay on the subject of *Nova Popularna* as part of
    this series.

Select Bibliography on Curators, Curating, and Exhibition Histories
Adorno, Theodor W. "Valéry Proust Museum." In *Prisms*, translated by Samuel Weber and Shirley
    Weber, 173-86. Cambridge, MA: MIT Press, 1981.
Alberro, Alexander. "Institutions, Critique, and Institutional Critique." In *Institutional
    Critique: An Anthology of Artists' Writings*. Edited by Alexander Alberro and Blake
    Stimson, 2-19. Cambridge, MA: MIT Press, 2009.
——. "The Silver Lining of Globalization: On 'Principio Potosí.'" *Texte zur Kunst* 79
    (September 2010).
Altshuler, Bruce. *The Avant-Garde in Exhibition: New Art in the 20th Century*. Los Angeles:
    University of California Press, 1998.
——. *Biennials and Beyond: Exhibitions That Made Art History, 1962-2002*. London: Phaidon, 2013.
——. *From Salon to Biennial: Exhibitions That Made Art History, Volume 1: 1863-1959*. London:
    Phaidon, 2008.
Amor, Monica. "On the Contingency of Modernity and the Persistence of Canons." In *Antinomies
    of Art and Culture: Modernity, Postmodernity, Contemporaneity*. Edited by Terry Smith,
    Okwui Enwezor, and Nancy Condee, 83-96. Durham, NC: Duke University Press, 2008.
Baker, George. "The Globalization of the False: A Response to Okwui Enwezor." *Documents* 23
    (Spring 2004): 20-25.
Bann, Stephen. "The Cabinet of Curiosities as a Model of Visual Display: A Note on the
    Genealogy of the Contemporary Art Museum." In *Definitions of Visual Culture: The New Art
    History Revisited*. Montreal: Musée d'Art Contemporain de Montréal, 1994.
Barker, Emma, ed. *Contemporary Culture of Display*. New Haven: Yale University Press, 1999.
Basualdo, Carlos. "The Unstable Institution." *Manifesta Journal* 2 (2003): 50-61.
Bennett, Tony. *The Birth of the Museum: History, Theory, Politics*. London: Routledge, 1995.
Berlo, Janet Catherine, and Ruth B. Philips, eds. "The Problematics of Collecting and Display,
    Part 1." Special issue, *Art Bulletin* LXXVII, no. 1 (March 1995).
Bezzola, Tobia, and Roman Kurkmeyer, eds. *Harald Szeemann: with by through because towards
    despite, Catalogue of All Exhibitions 1957-2005*. Zürich: Edition Voldemeer, 2007.
Boersma, Linda S. *0,10: The Last Futurist Exhibition of Painting*. Rotterdam: 010
    Publishers, 1994.
Bois, Yve-Alain. "Exposition: Esthétique de la distraction, espace de démonstration."
    Les Cahiers du Musée national d'art moderne 29 (Autumn 1989): 57-79.

Bojan, Maria Rus, Beatrice von Bismarck, Liam Gillick, Jens Hoffmann, Adam Kleinman, Sohrab
     Mohebbi, Nato Thompson, Vivian Rehberg, Dorothee Richter, Jacopo Crivelli Visconti, and
     Tirdad Zolghadr. "Letters to the Editors: Eleven Responses to Anton Vidokle's 'Art Without
     Artists.'" *e-flux journal* 18 (September 2010). Accessible at: http://www.e-flux.com/
     journal/letters-to-the-editors-eleven-responses-to-anton-vidokle's-"art-without-artists".
Bollé, Michael, and Eva Züchner, eds. *Stationen der moderne: Die bedeutenden Kunstaussellungen
     des 20. Jarhunderts in Deutschland.* Berlin: Berlinische Galerie, 1988. Exhibition catalogue.
Bonk, Ecke. *Marcel Duchamp: The Portable Museum.* London: Thames and Hudson, 1989.
Bright, Deborah. "Shopping the Leftovers: Warhol's Collecting Strategies in 'Raid the Icebox
     I.'" *Art History* 24, no. 2 (April 2001): 278-291.
Bronson, A.A., and Peggy Gale, eds. *Museums by Artists.* Toronto: Art Metropole, 1983.
Buchloh, Benjamin H.D. "Conceptual Art 1962-1969: From the Aesthetic of Administration to the
     Critique of Institutions." *October* 55 (Winter 1990): 105-143.
——. "The Museum Fictions of Marcel Broodthaers." In *Museums by Artists.* Edited by A.A. Bronson
     and Peggy Gale, 45-56. Toronto: Art Metropole, 1983.
Buchman, Sabeth. "Who's Afraid of Exhibiting?" In *unExhibit.* Edited by Sabine Folie and Lise
     Lafer, 176-177. Vienna: Generali Foundation, 2011.
Buren, Daniel. "Critical Limits." *Five Text* 38 (1970). Reprint, New York: John Weber Gallery,
     1974.
——. "The Function of the Exhibition." *Studio International* 186, no. 961 (December 1973): 216.
——. "Function of the Museum." *Artforum* 12, no. 1 (September 1973): 68.
——. "The Function of the Studio." In *Institutional Critique: An Anthology of Artists'
     Writings.* Edited by Alexander Alberro and Blake Stimson, 110-119. 1971. Reprint,
     Cambridge, MA: MIT Press, 2011.
Butler, Cornelia, ed. *From Conceptualism to Feminism: Lucy Lippard's Numbers Shows 1969-74.*
     London: Afterall, 2012.
Celant, Germano, and Chiara Costa, eds. *When Attitudes Become Form: Bern 1969/Venice 2013.*
     Milan: Fondazione Prada, 2013.
Chan, Carsten. "Measures of an Exhibition: Space, Not Art, Is the Curator's Primary
     Material." *Fillip* 13 (Spring 2011). Accessible at: http://fillip.ca/content/
     measures-of-an-exhibition.
Cooke, Lynn, and Peter Wollen, eds. *Visual Display: Culture Beyond Appearances.* New York and
     Seattle: Dia Art Foundation and Bay Press, 1995.
Corrin, Lisa G. "Mining the Museum: Confronting History in the Museum." *Curator* 36, no. 4
     (December 1993): 302-313.
Crimp, Douglas. *On the Museum's Ruins.* Cambridge, MA: MIT Press, 1993.
——. "This Is Not a Museum of Art." In *Marcel Broodthaers.* Minneapolis and New York: Walker Art
     Center and Rizzoli, 1989.
Decter, Joshua. "De-Coding the Museum." *FlashArt* 23, no. 155 (November-December 1990): 140-142.
Derieux, Florence, ed. *Harald Szeemann: Individual Methodology.* Zürich: JRP Ringier, 2007.
Duncan, Carol. "Museum of Modern Art as Late Capitalist Ritual: An Iconographic Analysis."
     Marxist Perspectives 1, no. 4 (Winter 1978): 28-51.
Dunlop, Ian. *The Shock of the New: Seven Historic Exhibitions of Modern Art.* New York: American
     Heritage, 1972.
Duro, Paul, ed. *The Rhetoric of the Frame: Essays on the Boundaries of the Artwork.* Cambridge,
     UK: Cambridge University Press, 1996.
Ekeberg, Jonas, ed. *New Institutionalism.* Oslo: OCA/verksted, 2003.
Enwezor, Okwui. "Mega-Exhibitions and the Antinomies of a Transnational Global Form." *Documents*
     23 (Spring 2004): 2-19.

Fairbrother, Trevor J. *The Label Show: Contemporary Art and the Museum*. Boston: Department of
Contemporary Art, Museum of Fine Arts, 1994.

Farquharson, Alex. "I curate, you curate, we curate." *Art Monthly* 269 (September 2003): 7–10.

Filipovic, Elena. "A Museum That Is Not." *e-flux journal* 4 (March 2009).

Filipovic, Elena, Marieke van Hal, and Solveig Øvstebo, eds. *The Biennial Reader: Anthology on
Large-Scale Perennial Exhibitions of Contemporary Art*. Bergen, Norway, and Ostfildern:
Bergen Kunsthall and Hatje Cantz, 2010.

Foster, Hal. "The Archive without Museums." *October 77* (Summer 1996): 97–119.

———. "Archives of Modern Art." *October* 99 (Winter 2002): 81–95.

Fraser, Andrea. "From the Critique of Institutions to an Institution of Critique." *Artforum* 44,
no. 1 (September 2005): 278–283. Reprinted in *Institutional Critique and After*. Edited by
John C. Welchman, 123–35. Zürich: JRP/Ringier, 2006.

———. "What Is Institutional Critique?" *Texte zur Kunst* (September 2005). Reprinted in
Institutional Critique and After. Edited by John C. Welchman, 305–309. Zürich: JRP/
Ringier, 2006.

Furján, Helene. "The Specular Spectacle of the House of the Collector." *Assemblage* 34
(1998): 56–91.

Gielen, Pascal, ed. "The Art Biennial as a Global Phenomenon: Strategies in Neo-Political
Times." Special issue of *Open* 16. Rotterdam: NAi Publishers, 2009.

Gleadowe, Teresa. "Inhabiting Exhibition History." *The Exhibitionist* 4 (June 2011): 29–34.

Gough, Maria. *The Artist as Producer: Russian Constructivism in Revolution*. Los Angeles:
University of California Press, 2005.

———. "Constructed Disoriented: El Lissitzky's Dresden and Hannover Demonstrationsräum."
In *Situating El Lissitzky: Vitebsk, Berlin, Moscow*. Edited by Nancy Perloff and
Brian Reed, 77–125. Los Angeles: Getty Research Institute, 2003.

———. "Futurist Museology." *Modernism/Modernity* 10, no. 2 (2003): 327–348.

Grace, Claire. "Counter-Time: Group Material's Chronicle of US Intervention in Central and
South America." *Afterall* 26 (Spring 2011). Accessible at: http://www.afterall.org/
journal/issue.26/counter-me-group-material-s-chronicle-of-us-intervention-in-central-and-
south-america.

Grasskamp, Walter. "Reviewing the Museum—or: The Complexity of Things." *Nordisk Museologi* 1
(1994): 65–74.

Gray, Zoë et al, eds. *Rotterdam Dialogues: The Critics, The Curators, The Artists*. Rotterdam:
Witte de With Publishers Post Editions, 2010.

Greenberg, Reesa, Bruce Ferguson, and Sandy Naire, eds. *Thinking About Exhibitions*. London
and New York: Routledge, 1996.

Gregos, Katerina. "MoMAS: The Unlikely Museum." In *Modell Martin Kippenberger: Utopien
für Alle*. Edited by Peter Pakesch, 68–83. Cologne: Verlag der Buchhandlung Walther
König, 2007.

Griffin, Tim, Francesco Bonami, Catherine David, Hans Ulrich Obrist, James Meyer, and Okwui
Enwezor. "Global Tendencies: Globalism and the Large-Scale Exhibition." *Artforum* 42, no. 3
(November 2003): 163–212.

Grigely, Joseph. *Exhibition Prosthetics*. London and Berlin: Bedford Press and Sternberg
Press, 2010.

Grunenberg, Christoph. "The Politics of Presentation: The Museum of Modern Art, New York."
In *Art Apart: Art Institutions and Ideology Across England and North America*. Edited by
Marcia Pointon. Manchester and New York: Manchester University Press, 1994.

Hoffman, Jens, ed. *The Next Documenta Should Be Curated by an Artist*. New York: e-flux/
Revolver, 2003.

———. *Ten Fundamental Questions of Curating*. Milan: Mousse Publishing, 2013.

Inkster, Dean. "Défense de la lecture: Le process de Pol Pot." In "Oublier l'Exposition."
    Special issue, *Art Press* 21 (2000): 64-69.

Kachur, Lewis. *Displaying the Marvelous: Duchamp, Dali, and the Surrealist Exhibitions.*
    Cambridge, MA: MIT Press, 2001.

Karp, Ivan, and Fred Wilson. "Constructing the Spectacle of Culture in Museums." *Art Papers*
    (May-June 1993): 2-9.

Karp, Ivan, and Stephen Lavine, eds. *Exhibiting Cultures: The Poetics and Politics of Museum
    Display.* Washington DC, and Cambridge, UK: Smithsonian Institute Press and Cambridge
    University Press, 1991.

Klonk, Charlotte. *Spaces of Experience: Art Gallery Interiors from 1800 to 2000.* New Haven and
    London: Yale University Press, 2009.

Klüser, Bernd, and Katharina Hegewisch, eds. *Die Kunst der Ausstellung: eine Dokumentation dreissig
    exemplarischer Kunstausstellungen dieses Jahrhunderts.* Frankfurt am Main: Insel, 1991.

Krauss, Rosalind. "The Cultural Logic of the Late Capitalist Museum." *October* 54
    (Autumn 1990): 3-17.

——. "Le Musée sans murs du Postmodernisme." "L'oeuvre et son accrochage." Special issue,
    Les Cahiers du Musée nationale d'art moderne, no. 17/18, (1986): 152-158.

Lawless, Catherine, ed. "L'oeuvre et son accrochage." Special issue, *Les Cahiers du Musée
    nationale d'art moderne,* no. 17/18 (1986).

Leguillon, Pierre, ed. "Oublier l'Exposition." Special issue, *Art Press* 21 (2000).

Mainardi, Patricia. "Courbet's Exhibitionism." *Gazette des Beaux-Arts* 118 (December 1991):
    253-266.

Malbert, Roger. "Artists as Curators." *Museum Journal* (May 1995): 25-26.

Marincola, Paula. *What Makes a Great Exhibition?* Philadelphia: University of the Arts,
    Philadelphia Exhibitions Initiative, 2007.

McDonald, Sharon, ed. *The Politics of Display: Museums, Science, Culture.* London and New York:
    Routledge, 1997.

McShine, Kynaston, ed. *The Museum as Muse: Artists Reflect.* New York: Museum of Modern Art, 2002.

Meyer, James. "Working Drawings and Other Visible Things on Paper Not Necessarily Meant to Be
    Viewed as Art." In *Conceptual Art: Theory, Myth and Practice.* Edited by Michael Corris.
    New York: Cambridge University Press, 2004.

Möntmann, Nina. "The Rise and Fall of New Institutionalism: Perspectives on a Possible Future."
    Transversal (August 2007). Accessible at: http://eipcp.net/transversal/0407/moentmann/en/.

——. "(Under) Privileged Spaces: On Martha Rosler's 'If You Lived Here . . .'"
    e-flux journal 9 (October 2009). Accessible at: http://www.e-flux.com/journal/
    underprivileged-spaces-on-martha-rosler%E2%80%99s-%E2%80%9Cif-you-lived-here-%E2%80%9D/.

Myers, Julian. "On the Value of a History of Exhibitions." *The Exhibitionist* 4
    (June 2011): 24-28.

Noyes Platt, Susan. "Modernism, Formalism, and Politics: The Cubism and Abstract Art Exhibition
    at the Museum of Modern Art." *Art Journal* 47, no. 4 (Winter 1988): 284-295.

Obrist, Hans Ulrich. *A Brief History of Curating.* Zürich: JRP Ringier, 2008.

——. *Everything You Always Wanted to Know About Curating But Were Afraid to Ask.* Berlin:
    Sternberg Press, 2011.

Ockman, Joan. "The Road Not Taken: Alexander Dorner's Way Beyond Art." In *Autonomy and
    Ideology: Positioning an Avant-garde in America.* Edited by Robert Somol. New York:
    Monacelli, 1997.

O'Doherty, Brian. *Inside the White Cube: The Ideology of the Gallery Space.* Santa Monica and
    San Francisco: Lapis Press, 1976.

——. *Studio and Cube: On the Relationship Between Where Art Is Made and Where Art Is Displayed.*
    New York: A FORuM Project Publication, 2007.

O'Neill, Paul. *The Culture of Curating, the Curating of Cultures.* Cambridge, MA:
    MIT Press, 2012.

O'Neill, Paul, ed. *Curating Subjects.* London: Open Editions, 2007.

O'Neill, Paul, and Mick Wilson, eds. *Curating and the Educational Turn.* London and Amsterdam:
    Open Editions and De Appel, 2010.

Perrodin, Roselyne Marsaud, ed. "Médiation: Propos sur l'exposition." Special issue, *Pratiques*
    3/4 (Autumn 1997).

Pierce, Sarah. "With Practicality Comes a Practice: The Artist as Curator." *Visual Artist
    Ireland.* Accessible at: http://visualartists.ie/advocacy/resources/infopool-2/
    professional-pathways/with-practicality-comes-a-practice-the-artist-as-curator/.

Poinsot, Jean-Marc. *L'atelier sans mur.* Villeurbanne: Art Edition, 1991.

——. "L'In situ et les circonstances de sa mise à vue." *Les Cahiers du Musée National d'Art
    Moderne*, no. 27 (Spring 1989): 67-75.

——. *Quand l'oeuvre a lieu: L'art exposé et ses recits autorisés.* Geneva and Villeurbanne:
    MAMCO-Institut d'Art Contemporaine and Institut d'art contemporain, 1999.

——. "La transformation du musée à l'ère de l'art exposé." *Traverses*, no. 36
    (January 1986): 42-49.

Preziosi, Donald. *Brain of the Earth's Body: Art, Museums, and the Phantasms of Modernity.*
    Minneapolis: University of Minnesota Press, 2003.

Putnam, James. *Art and Artifact: The Museum as Medium.* New York: Thames and Hudson, 2001.

Rajchman, John. "Les Immatériaux or How to Construct the History of Exhibitions."
    Tate Papers 12 (October 2009).

Raqs Media Collective. "Earthworms Dancing: Notes for a Biennial in Slow Motion."
    e-flux journal 7 (June 2009). Accessible at: http://www.e-flux.com/journal/
    earthworms-dancing-notes-for-a-biennial-in-slow-motion/.

Rattemeyer, Christian. "What History of Exhibitions?" *The Exhibitionist* 4 (June 2011): 35-41.

Rattemeyer, Christian, ed. *Exhibiting New Art: Op Losse Schroeven and When Attitudes Become
    Form, 1969.* London: Afterall, 2010.

Richter, Dorothee. "Artists and Curators as Authors—Competitors, Collaborators, or Team-
    Workers?" *On-Curating Journal* 19 (June 2013). Accessible at: http://oncurating-journal.
    de/files/oc/dateiverwaltung/issue-19/Print_to_download/ONCURATING_Issue19_A4.pdf.

——. "A Brief Outline of the History of Exhibition Making." *On-Curating Journal* 6 (2010).
    Accessible at: http://oncurating-journal.de/index.php/issue-6.html#. UnPm04Ulxkg.

Roberts, Catsou, and Timothy Landers, eds. *The Desire of the Museum.* New York: Whitney Museum
    of American Art, 1989.

Rogoff, Irit. "Turning." *e-flux journal* 0 (November 2008). Accessible at: http://www.e-flux.
    com/journal/turning/.

Rugg, Judith, and Michele Sedgwick, eds. *Issues in Curating Contemporary Art and Performance.*
    Bristol and Chicago: Intellect, 2007.

Schjeldahl, Peter. "Selective Affinities: The Artist as Curator." *The New Yorker* (September
    1999): 86-87.

Semin, Didier, and Isabelle Ewig. "Comment se fait une exposition?" *Les Cahiers du Musée
    National d'Art Moderne*, no. 73 (Autumn 2000): 4-35.

Sheikh, Simon. "Notes on Institutional Critique." *EIPCP. European Institute for Progressive
    Cultural Politics* (2006). Accessible at: http://eipcp.net/transversal/0106/ sheikh/en.

Sherman, Daniel, and Irit Rogoff, eds. *Museum Culture: Histories, Discourses, Spectacles.*
    Minneapolis: University of Minnesota Press, 1994.

Smith, Terry. *Thinking Contemporary Curating.* New York: International Curators International,
    2012.

Smithson, Robert, and Allan Kaprow. "What Is a Museum?" In *Robert Smithson: Collected Writings*. Edited by Jack Flam, 43-51. Berkeley: UC Press, 1996.

Stafford, Barbara Maria. "Voyeur or Observer? Enlightenment Thoughts on the Dilemmas of Display." *Configurations* 1, no. 1 (Winter 1993).

Staniszewski, Mary Anne. *The Power of Display: A History of Exhibition Installations at the Museum of Modern Art*. Cambridge, MA: MIT Press, 1998.

Steeds, Lucy, ed. *Making Art Global (Part 2): 'Magiciens de la Terre' 1989*. London: Afterall, 2013.

Steyerl, Hito. "Is the Museum a Factory?" *e-flux journal* 7 (June 2009). Accessible at: http://www.e-flux.com/journal/is-a-museum-a-factory/.

Tannert, Christoph, and Ute Tischler, eds. *MIB-Men in Black: Handbook of Curatorial Practice*. Berlin and Frankfurt am Main, 2004.

Valery, Paul. "Le problème des musées." In *Oeuvres complètes, vol. II: 1290-1293*. Paris: Bibliothèque de la Pléiade, 1923.

Vanderlinden, Barbara, and Elena Filipovic, eds. *The Manifesta Decade: Debates on Contemporary Art Exhibitions and Biennials in Post-Wall Europe*. Brussels and Cambridge, MA: Roomade and MIT Press, 2005.

Vergo, Peter. *The New Museology*. London: Reaktion Books, 1989.

Vidokle, Anton. "Art without Artists?" *e-flux journal* 16 (May 2010). Accessible at: http://www.e-flux.com/journal/art-without-artists/.

Vogel, Sabine. *Biennials: Art on a Global Scale*. Vienna: Springer, 2010.

Von Bismarck, Beatrice, Jörn Schafaff, and Thomas Weski, eds. *Cultures of the Curatorial*. Berlin and New York: Sternberg Press, 2012.

Von Hantlemann, Dorothea. "The Curatorial Paradigm." *The Exhibitionist* 4 (June 2011): 6-12.

——. *How to Do Things with Art*. Zürich and Dijon: JRP-Ringier/Les Presses du Réel, 2010.

——. "The Rise of the Exhibition and the Exhibition as Art." In *Aesthetics and Contemporary Art*. Edited by Armen Avanessian and Luke Skrebowski. Berlin: Sternberg Press, 2011.

Von Hantlemann, Dorothea, and Carolin Meister, eds. *Die Ausstellung: Politik eines Rituals*. Berlin and Zürich: Diaphanes, 2010.

Wallach, Alan. "The Museum of Modern Art: The Past's Future." *Journal of Design History* 5, no. 3 (1992): 207-215. Accessible at: http://www.jstor.org/over/10.2307/1315838?uid=3737864&uid=2129&uid=2&uid=70&uid=4&sid=21102869046923.

Wallenstein, Sven-Olav. "The Site of the Work of Art." *MLN* 109, no. 3 (Spring 1994): 478-494.

Ward, Frazer. "The Haunted Museum: Institutional Critique and Publicity." *October* 73 (Summer 1995): 71-89.

Weiss, Rachel, ed. *Making Art Global (Part 1): The Third Havana Biennial 1989*. London: Afterall, 2011.

See also the following journals devoted to curating:

Cura, Curator, Journal of Curatorial Studies, On Curating.org Journal, Manifesta Journal, and *The Exhibitionist*.

This essay was originally published in *The Artist as Curator* #0, insert in *Mousse* 41. Parts of this essay were first given as a keynote address at the 2012 conference Artist as Curator, organized by Afterall. The author especially thanks Pablo Lafuente and Charles Esche for the invitation to reflect on this larger project there.

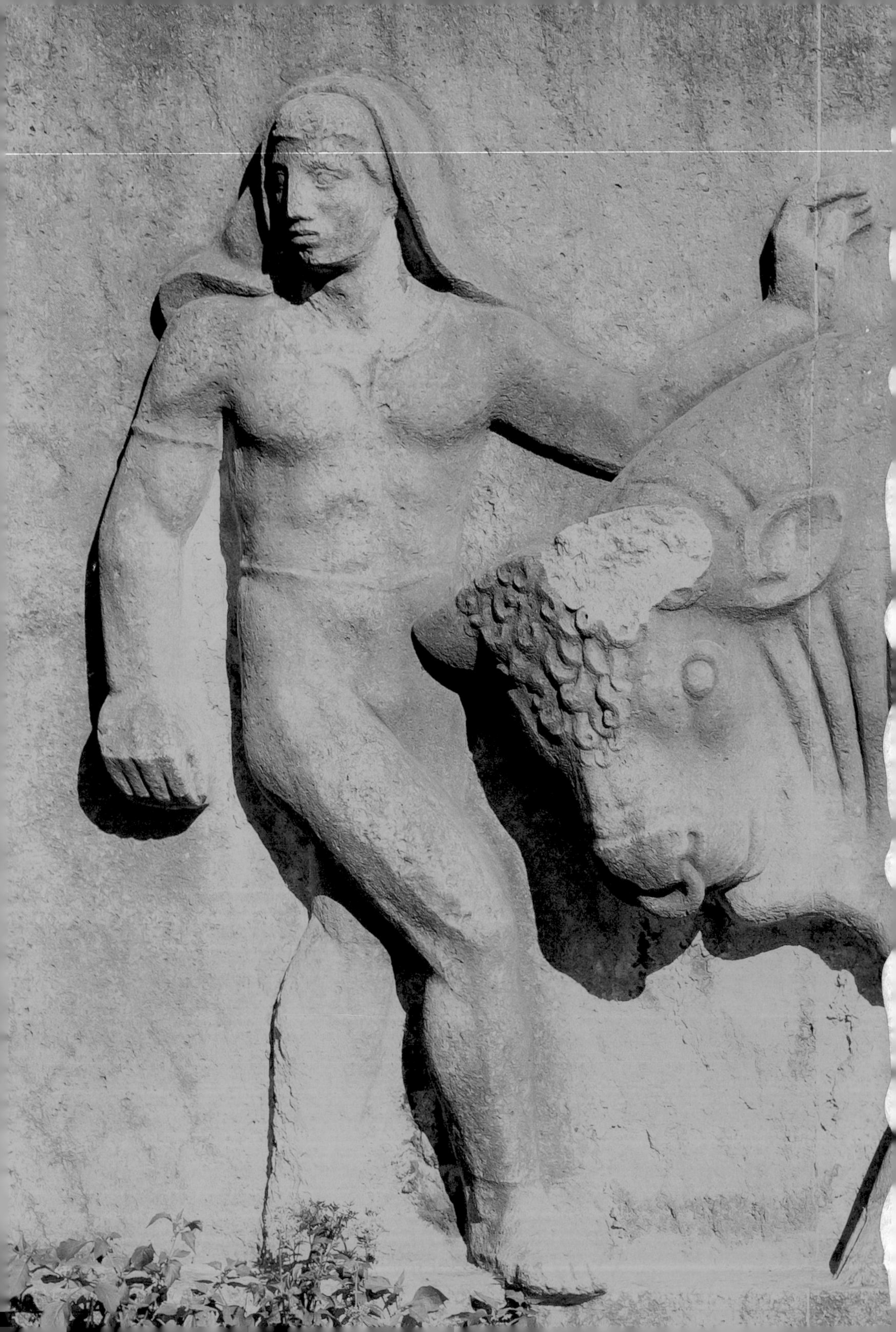

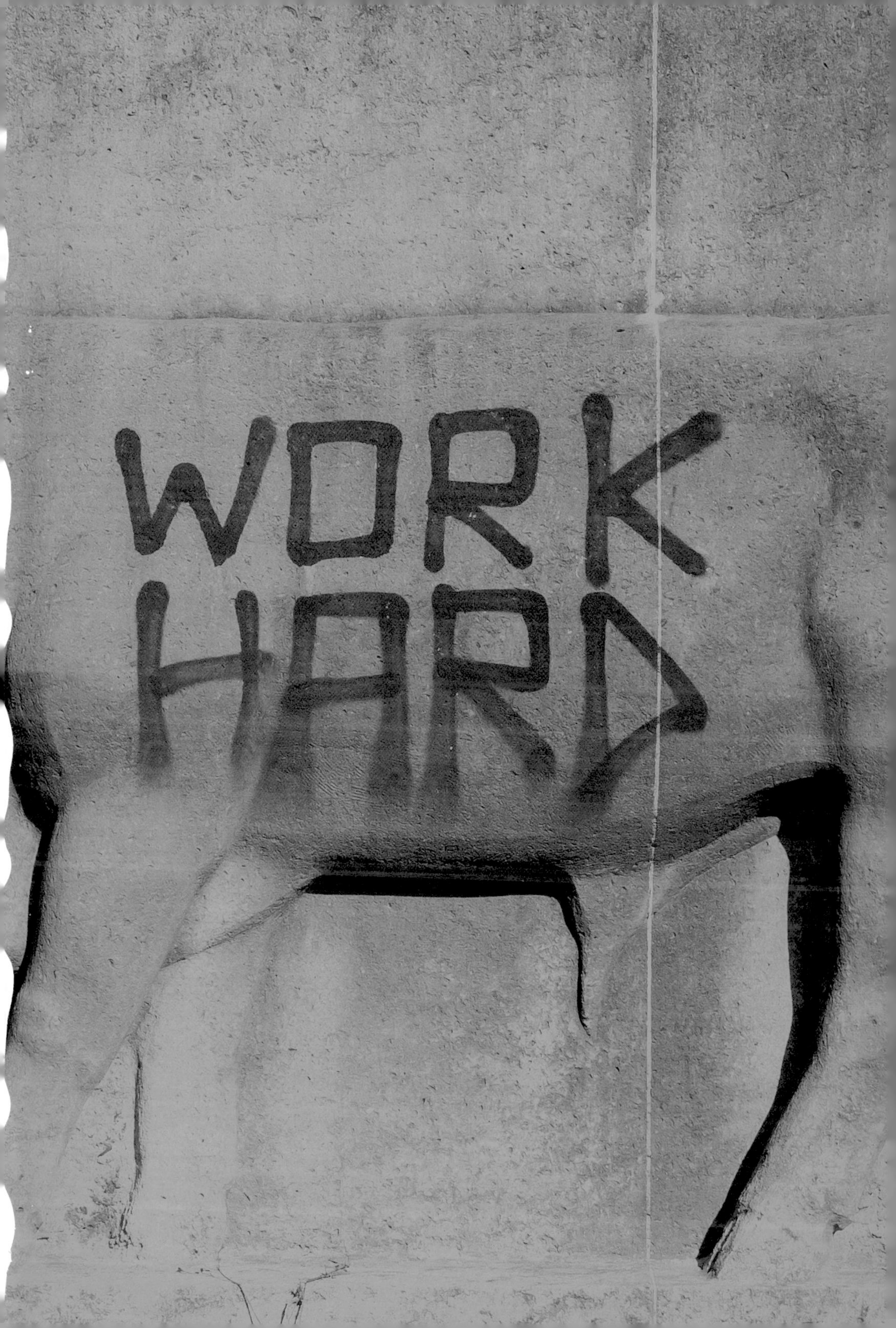

WORK
HARD

Works

EDMOND BILLE
Une danse macabre, 1919
Folio book
19¾ × 13¾ × ¾ inches
Private collection, Martigny
pp. 11–14

VITTORIO BRODMANN
Untitled, 2013
Oil on canvas
24 × 31½ inches
Private collection, Martigny
pp. 69, 71

MARGUERITE BURNAT-PROVINS
Asclibour entoure, 1929
Pencil and watercolor
18 × 15¼ inches
Courtesy of the Collection
de l'Art Brut, Lausanne
pp. 40, 45, 82

MARGUERITE BURNAT-PROVINS
Cenio L'abruti!, 1934
Pencil and watercolor
7 × 5 inches
Courtesy of the Collection
de l'Art Brut, Lausanne
pp. 40, 42

MARGUERITE BURNAT-PROVINS
Coquetterie, 1932
Watercolor
13½ × 15½ inches
Courtesy of the Collection
de l'Art Brut, Lausanne
pp. 40, 46, 82

MARGUERITE BURNAT-PROVINS
Croix le désagréable, 1916
Pencil and watercolor
9½ × 10½ inches
Courtesy of the Collection
de l'Art Brut, Lausanne
pp. 40, 43, 108

MARGUERITE BURNAT-PROVINS
Frilute le peureux, 1915
Pencil and watercolor
13 × 14½ inches
Courtesy of the Collection
de l'Art Brut, Lausanne
pp. 41, 49, 82

MARGUERITE BURNAT-PROVINS
Hanugre et le chat, 1919
Pencil and watercolor
18 × 13 inches
Courtesy of the Collection
de l'Art Brut, Lausanne
pp. 40, 44, 82

MARGUERITE BURNAT-PROVINS
La curiosité, 1935
Pencil and ink
10 × 14½ inches
Courtesy of the Collection
de l'Art Brut, Lausanne
pp. 41, 48, 82

MARGUERITE BURNAT-PROVINS
La tête qui se balance, 1917
Pencil and watercolor
15½ × 23 inches
Courtesy of the Collection
de l'Art Brut, Lausanne
pp. 41, 47, 82

MARGUERITE BURNAT-PROVINS
La vie est-ce bon?, undated
Pencil and watercolor
12 × 8½ inches
Courtesy of the Collection
de l'Art Brut, Lausanne
pp. 41, 50, 82

MARGUERITE BURNAT-PROVINS
Mauglu Professeur, 1918
Pencil and watercolor
6 × 7¾ inches
Courtesy of the Collection
de l'Art Brut, Lausanne
pp. 41, 51, 82

LUCIANO CASTELLI
Brücke, 1994
Bronze
8 × 27¾ × 16½ inches
Edition 2/5
Courtesy the artist
pp. 73, 78, 80-81, 83

CLAUDIA COMTE
Lapin africain 5, 2014
Cedar, metal, and car lacquer
Dimensions variable
Courtesy the artist
pp. 67-68

SYLVAIN CROCI-TORTI
Lost in Confusion, 2014
Acrylic on canvas
47¼ × 59¼ inches
Courtesy the artist
pp. 25, 53

LATIFA ECHAKHCH
Skin, 2012
Shoes
Dimensions variable
Courtesy the artist and
Kaufmann Repetto, Milan
pp. 16-17, 72

FRÉDÉRIC GABIOUD
Untitled, 2012
Acrylic on canvas
40¾ × 4 × 1 inches
Private collection, Martigny
p. 89

MATHIS GASSER
*Superstructures
for Europe*, 2012
Acrylic on canvas
14 × 10 inches
Private collection, Martigny
pp. 25, 37, 39

FABRICE GYGI
Tente-Bar, 1997
Metal, wood, tarpaulin,
leather, neon, and plexiglass
98½ × 78¾ × 78¾ inches
Courtesy of the artist and
FCAC, Republic and Canton
of Geneva
pp. 54, 74-75

TRIX AND ROBERT HAUSSMANN
Neon Chair, 1967
Fluorescent bulbs and fur
23¾ × 23¾ × 39½ inches
Courtesy the artists
pp. 75, 77

ANDREAS HOCHULI
Pfäffikon/SZ, 2014
Acrylic on canvas
35½ × 28 inches
Private collection, Martigny
pp. 83, 85

DAVID HOMINAL
Animal with Baggage, 2010
Mixed media
8½ × 2½ × 4¾ inches
Courtesy the artist and
Galerie Kamel Mennour, Paris
pp. 28, 35

DAVID HOMINAL
Ni le soleil ni la mort, 2011
Mixed media
9½ × 4¾ × 3½ inches
Courtesy the artist and
Galerie Kamel Mennour, Paris
pp. 20, 28, 31

DAVID HOMINAL
ST070910, 2010
Mixed media
8 × 4¾ × 3½ inches
Courtesy the artist and
Galerie Kamel Mennour, Paris
pp. 28, 34

DAVID HOMINAL
ST070910-II, 2010
Mixed media
10 × 6¾ × 5 inches
Courtesy the artist and
Galerie Kamel Mennour, Paris
pp. 20, 28, 33

BERNHARD LUGINBÜHL
*Modell zum Karlsruher
Stengel*, 1968
Iron
40¾ × 33½ × 13 inches
Courtesy of Galerie
Von Bartha, Basel
p. 20

URS LÜTHI
*Some day when my longing is
gone, I'm gonna take a smile
for a walk in the sun*, 1975
Artist book
34 pages, 9¼ × 9 inches
Courtesy of Phil Aarons
and Shelley Fox Aarons
pp. 56-65

FABIAN MARTI
*Amber and Green Egg with 10
Breeding Ouroboroi*, 2014
Polyester
47 × 68¾ inches
Courtesy the artist and
Peter Kilchmann, Zürich
pp. 38, 73

MÉRET OPPENHEIM
Traccia Table, 1972
Bronze and plywood
27¼ × 21 × 25 inches
Courtesy of Liz O'Brien,
New York
pp. 39, 73, 82

SIMON PACCAUD
Crocodile, 2012
Caps, crowbars, canes,
and lace
118¼ × 59¼ × 1¼ inches
Courtesy the artist
pp. 25, 72

MAI-THU PERRET
Black Balthazar, 2013
Birch plywood, rattan core,
and water-based paint
48½ × 45½ × 12 inches
Private collection
pp. 9, 90, 92

UGO RONDINONE
achternovemberzweitausendund-
vierzehn, 2014
Acrylic on canvas, plexiglass
plaque with caption
270 × 180 × 3 inches
Courtesy the artist and
Galerie Eva Presenhuber,
Zürich
pp. 6, 20, 26, 29, 75

DENIS SAVARY
Alma (After Kokoschka), 2007
Mixed media
64¼ × 29¾ × 12¾ inches
Courtesy of MAMCO (Musée d'art
moderne et contemporain),
Geneva
pp. 87, 98

DANIEL SPOERRI
Le danger de la
multiplication, 1971
Mixed media
39½ × 39½ × 4 inches
Courtesy of Andres Jllien
pp. 19, 74, 114

JEAN TINGUELY
Peut-être No. 11, ca. 1959
Metal mobile relief, motorized
24 × 19¾ × 8 inches
Courtesy of Albright-Knox Art
Gallery, Buffalo, New York
pp. 9, 21-3, 72, 91

Artist Biographies

EDMOND BILLE was born in 1858 in Valangin, Switzerland. He died in 1959 in Sierre, Switzerland.

MARGUERITE BURNAT-PROVINS was born in 1872 in Arras, France. She died in 1952 in Grasse, France.

VITTORIO BRODMANN was born in 1987 in Ettingen, Switzerland. He lives and works in Zürich and Vienna.

LUCIANO CASTELLI was born in 1951 in Lucerne, Switzerland. He lives and works in Zürich, Paris, and Normandy.

CLAUDIA COMTE was born in 1983 in Grancy, Switzerland. She lives and works in Berlin.

SYLVAIN CROCI-TORTI lives and works in Lausanne, Switzerland.

LATIFA ECHAKHCH was born in 1974 in El Khnansa, Morocco. She lives and works in Martigny, Switzerland.

FRÉDÉRIC GABIOUD was born in 1990 in Lausanne, Switzerland, where he currently lives and works.

MATHIS GASSER was born in 1984 in Zürich. He lives and works in London.

FABRICE GYGI was born in 1965 in Geneva, where he currently lives and works.

TRIX HAUSSMANN was born in 1933 in Chur, Switzerland. ROBERT HAUSSMANN was born in 1931 in Zürich. They have worked together in Zürich since 1976.

ANDREAS HOCHULI was born in 1982 in Switzerland. He lives and works in Leipzig, Germany.

DAVID HOMINAL was born in 1976 in France. He lives and works in Berlin.

BERNHARD LUGINBÜHL was born in 1929 in Bern, Switzerland.
He died in 2011.

URS LÜTHI was born in 1947 in Zürich. He lives and works
in Munich.

FABIAN MARTI was born in 1979 in Fribourg, Switzerland.
He lives and works in Zürich.

MÉRET OPPENHEIM was born in 1913 in Berlin. She died in
1985 in Basel, Switzerland.

SIMON PACCAUD was born in 1985. He lives and works in
Lausanne, Switzerland.

MAI-THU PERRET was born in 1976 in Geneva, where she lives
and works. She contributed an untitled essay to this book.

UGO RONDINONE was born in 1964 in Brunnen, Switzerland.
He lives and works in New York.

DENIS SAVARY was born in 1981 in Granges-près-Marnand,
Switzerland. He lives and works in Geneva.

DANIEL SPOERRI was born in 1930 in Galați, Romania.
He lives and works in Vienna.

JEAN TINGUELY was born in 1925 in Fribourg, Switzerland.
He died in 1991 in Bern, Switzerland.

Contributor Biographies

VALENTIN CARRON lives and works in Martigny, Switzerland, where he was born in 1977. In 2013 he represented Switzerland at the 55th Venice Biennale. Major presentations of his works were realized at Kunsthalle Bern (2014); Palais de Tokyo, Paris (2010); Kunsthalle Zürich (2007); Swiss Institute, New York (2006); Centre d'Art Contemporain, Geneva (2004); Chisenhale Gallery, London (2006); and MAMCO, Geneva (2001). Catalogues were published on the occasion of Carron's exhibition at the Swiss Pavilion for the 55th International Venice Biennale (JRP-Ringier) and his recent solo exhibition at Kunsthalle Bern. A monograph of the artist's work was published by JRP-Ringier in 2011.

ELENA FILIPOVIC is director and chief curator of Kunsthalle Basel. She was senior curator at WIELS Contemporary Art Centre, Brussels, from 2009 to 2014. She cocurated the 5th Berlin Biennial (2008) with Adam Szymczyk, and coedited *The Biennial Reader: An Anthology on Large-Scale Perennial Exhibitions of Contemporary Art* (2010), with Marieke van Hal and Solveig Øvstebø. She has curated a number of traveling retrospectives, including *Anne Teresa De Keersmaeker: Work/Travail/Arbeid* (2015); *Mark Leckey: Lending Enchantment to Vulgar Materials* (2014); *Franz Erhard Walther: The Body Decides* (2014); *Alina Szapocznikow: Sculpture Undone, 1955-1972*, cocurated with Joanna Mytkowska (2011-12); and *Felix Gonzalez-Torres: Specific Objects without Specific Form* (2010-11), in addition to organizing solo exhibitions with emerging artists such as Zhana Ivanova, Petrit Halilaj, Leigh Ledare, Klara Lidén, and Tris Vonna-Michell. Filipovic's writings have appeared in numerous artists' catalogues and journals, and she is editor of the serial publication *The Artist as Curator* for *Mousse*.

BORIS GROYS is Professor of Aesthetics, Art History, and Media Theory at the Center for Art and Media Karlsruhe and Global Distinguished Professor at New York University. He is the author of many books, including *The Total Art of Stalinism* (1992), *Politique de l'immortalité: Quatre entretien avec Thomas Knoefel* (2005), *Ilya Kabakov: The Man Who Flew into Space from His Apartment* (2006), *Art Power* (2008), *The Communist Postscript* (2010), and *Going Public* (2010).

BALTHAZAR LOVAY is a Swiss artist and curator. He is currently the artistic director of Fri Art, Centre d'art de Fribourg in Switzerland, where he has organized solo exhibitions by artists such as Ramaya Tegegne, Cameron Rowland, Kathe Burkhart, Ferdinand Kriwet, and Robert Heinecken. He has also included programs of experimental cinema and experimental music, with concerts by Keiji Haino, Junko Hiroshige, Michael Gendreau, and Peter Rehberg, among others. His own work has been exhibited at AP News, Zürich; Burning Bridges, Brooklyn; Galerie Francesca Pia, Zürich; and New Jerseyy, Basel. Along with Mathieu Copeland, he is the coeditor of the forthcoming anthology *Anti-Museum*, which will be released by Walther König, Cologne in 2016.

MAI-THU PERRET is an artist and writer who lives in Geneva. She is known for her multidisciplinary practice encompassing sculpture, painting, video, and installation. Perret has created a complex oeuvre that combines radical feminist politics with literary texts, homemade crafts, and twentieth-century avant-garde aesthetics. Her recent solo shows have appeared at the Nasher Sculpture Center, Dallas (2016); Le Magasin, Grenoble, France (2011); MAMCO, Geneva (2011); Aargauer Kunsthaus, Aarau, Switzerland (2011); and Swiss Institute, New York (2011). Her work has been featured in numerous group shows as well, including at the Musée d'Art Moderne, Paris (2013); Centre Pompidou, Paris (2012); Kunsthalle Bern, Switzerland (2012); *ILLUMInations* (curated by Bice Curiger), 54th Venice Biennale (2011); and Haus der Kunst, Munich (2010).

Acknowledgments

First and foremost, I must thank the unique, brilliant mind behind *Work Hard*: Valentin Carron. His enthusiasm for the project, and his consummate curatorial ingenuity, made the production of this exhibition an immensely rewarding experience.

I am deeply grateful to Elena Filipovic, Boris Groys, Balthazar Lovay, and Mai-Thu Perret for contributing to this book. Their insights into Valentin's curatorial debut, along with broader themes of the artist as curator, imbue the exhibition with perceptive depth.

Additionally, Swiss Institute would like to warmly thank all participants in the public programs throughout this exhibition, including, in order of appearance: Claudia Comte, Mai-Thu Perret, Fabrice Stroun, Elena Filipovic, Jennifer Chan, Josh Kline, Leah Schrager, Boris Groys, Andreas Angelidakis, Marie Karlberg, and Lena Henke.

Realizing this exhibition would not have been possible without the generosity of our lenders. Therefore, I would like to express my gratitude to Phil Aarons and Shelley Fox Aarons; the Albright-Knox Art Gallery, Buffalo; Collection de l'Art Brut, Lausanne; Galerie Eva Presenhuber, Zürich; Galerie Gregor Staiger, Zürich; Galerie Kamel Mennour, Paris; Galerie Peter Kilchmann, Zürich; von Bartha, Basel; Andreas Illien; FCAC, Republic and Canton of Geneva; Kaufmann Repetto, Milan; Liz O'Brien, New York; MAMCO (Musée d'art moderne et contemporain), Geneva; and the Marciano Art Collection, Los Angeles.

Special thanks must be given to 303 Gallery, David Kordansky Gallery, Kamel Mennour, and Galerie Eva Presenhuber for their crucial support to the development of the exhibition. Swiss Institute is also grateful to agnès b., with whom Valentin collaborated on a special edition tote bag commemorating the exhibition.

I would be remiss if I did not thank our editor Karen Marta and Christopher Impiglia for their invaluable editorial insights and commitment to books of the highest quality. As with the first four books in the SI Series, I am especially grateful to Brendan Dugan, Sinisa Mackovic, Elizabeth Karp-Evans, David Schoerner, and Nicholas Weltyk of Karma, whose remarkable skill, boundless patience, and generosity were essential in realizing this publication.

The publication of this book was enabled by generous donations from David Kordansky Gallery and Galerie Eva Presenhuber. Both galleries have demonstrated a commitment to Valentin's artistic development, and their support of his inaugural foray into curating is a testament to their willingness to champion experimentation.

And, as always, I must express my gratitude to the Swiss Institute Board of Trustees, whose enthusiasm and desire to constantly expand our scope has ushered Swiss Institute into a new era. I would also like to thank the team at SI—especially Alison Coplan, Elizabeth Baribeau, Laura McLean-Ferris, and Daniel Merritt—for their dedicated, spirited efforts in bringing this publication to fruition.

Simon Castets

Swiss Institute

Founded in 1986, Swiss Institute is an independent, nonprofit contemporary art institution dedicated to promoting forward-thinking and experimental art-making through innovative exhibitions and programs. Committed to the highest standards of curatorial and educational excellence, Swiss Institute serves as a platform for emerging artists, catalyzes new contexts for celebrated work, and fosters appreciation for under-recognized positions.

Swiss Institute programming is made possible in part with public funds from Pro Helvetia, Swiss Arts Council, the New York State Council on the Arts, with the support of Governor Andrew Cuomo and the New York State Legislature, and the New York City Department of Cultural Affairs in partnership with the City Council. Main Sponsors include LUMA Foundation, the Andy Warhol Foundation for the Visual Arts, and Friends of Swiss Institute (FOSI). Leading Partners include UBS and Victorinox. Swiss Institute gratefully acknowledges Stella Artois as Benefactor, Swiss Re as Public Programs Sponsor, and SWISS as Travel Partner.

The SI Series

Embracing the conceptual framework of an exhibition at Swiss Institute and its related public programs, each book in the SI Series adds retrospective context through seminal essays, archival materials, event transcripts, artist portfolios, and exhibition documentation, as well as reprints and new translations of important texts.

OTHER TITLES IN THE SI SERIES

Allyson Vieira: The Plural Present
Heidi Bucher
The St. Petersburg Paradox
Fin de Siècle
David Weiss: Works, 1968-1979
Niele Toroni
PAVILLON DE L'ESPRIT NOUVEAU: A 21st Century Show Home
Hans Schärer: Madonnas and Erotic Watercolors
FADE IN: INT. ART GALLERY - DAY
Sam Lewitt: Less Light Warm Words

Published for the exhibition
*Work Hard: Selections by
Valentin Carron* at
Swiss Institute, New York,
March 4–May 24, 2016

Editors:
Karen Marta, Simon Castets
Associate Editor:
Alison Coplan
Managing Editor:
Christopher Impiglia
Editorial Assistants:
Artrit Bytyçi, Daniel Merritt
Copy Editor: Michael Lacoy
Proofreader: Madeline Coleman
Photographer: Daniel Pérez
Initial design concept by
Studio Marie Lusa

SI staff for *Work Hard:
Selections by Valentin Carron*:
Simon Castets, Elizabeth
Baribeau, Clément Delépine,
Alison Coplan, Anastasia
Charaf, Alexandra Zigrang,
Daniel Merritt, Scott Kiernan,
Markee Speyer, Alex LoRe,
Lisa Hamilton
Volunteers: Milena Burge,
Sarah Hibbs, Jin Noh, Martina
Olivetti, Katherine Raber, Max
Smith-Holmes, Maurice Ziegler
Installers: John McLaughlin,
Donals D'Aries, Victor De
Matha, Giles Hefferan

Swiss Institute
www.swissinstitute.net

Karma, New York
www.karmakarma.org

Available through
D.A.P. / Distributed Art
Publishers, Inc.
155 6th Avenue, 2nd Floor
New York, NY 10013
Tel: +1 212 627 1999
www.artbook.com

This book was made possible
in part by generous support
from David Kordansky Gallery
and Galerie Eva Presenhuber.

Printed in Poland

ISBN: 978-1-942607-27-4

Cristina Bechtler &
Dora Imhof [eds.]
*The Private Museum
of the Future*

JRP|RINGIER & LES PRESSES DU RÉEL